He Outlived His Smile

Stanley Ingram

Dedication

I dedicate this story to every man, woman, and child whose spirit has been crushed by the cruelty of war.

Contents

Chapter 1 - Going to Work

On a cold Saturday morning, Joel was awakened by his mother earlier than his usual time, interrupting his cozy sleep. As he rubbed his eyes and looked at the clock, he saw that it was 5:30 in the morning. Despite feeling tired and groggy from the lost hour of sleep, Joel got out of bed and sleepily put on his good overalls, and picked up his brogans. He walked towards the front room, which served as the kitchen, dining room, and his parent's bedroom. Excited for his first day of third grade, Joel had carefully laid out his clothes and shoes the night before and was looking forward to skipping his regular morning task of gathering kindling for the house and going straight to school after breakfast.

However, as soon as Joel entered the room, he could sense a heavy atmosphere. His mother's eyes were a deep pink, possibly from crying, and his father, Hubert Mills, watched him with sympathetic eyes. Confused and unsure of what was happening, Joel walked over to his parent's bed near the red brick fireplace and sat down to tie his hand-me-down shoes. But before he could lace them up, his father spoke, "Joel, you won't be needing those today. Put them away and put on your work bibs." His father's words caught Joel off guard and added to the confusion and uncertainty he was feeling.

As Joel stood there, his back slightly bent and his hands holding the laces of his shoes, the weight of his father's words hit him like a freight train. He could feel the disappointment and confusion wash over him as he processed what his father had said. His mother, standing beside a dining table chair, broke into quiet sobs, her hand placed over her mouth and the other on the table for support.

"But dad," Joel said after a short pause, "I start third grade this morning, and little Bert starts first!" His father could sense the disappointment in his calm protest, so he moved a little closer to where Joel was. Hubert said, "Your brothers can't keep up with things around here while I'm working in town, and it's high time you start pulling your weight around here."

Before Joel could fully grasp the situation and respond, his younger brother, Bert, spoke up. "Dad, if my brothers have to work, then so should I. I ain't going to school, either!" Their mother quickly moved to Bert's side and sat beside him. With a breaking voice, she said, "No, son, you have to learn to read and," but before she could finish her sentence, Hubert cut her off by saying, "If the boy doesn't want to go to school, we ain't forcing him. Besides, we could use the help around here."

At that moment, all of the excitement and anticipation that Joel had felt for the start of the school year vanished. He could almost see it disappearing into thin air. Joel loved reading, and he loved mathematics more than any other boy he knew, but he couldn't afford to keep his father waiting. He knew very well that any delay might result in a belt across his back. So, with his head hanging low, he simply nodded and left the big room, his dreams and aspirations for the future crushed.

As it turns out, the saying "time heals everything" holds true; even if it doesn't completely heal, it at least makes things less difficult. In the two days following his father's decision to make him quit school, the sting of giving up his dreams began to soften for Joel. He discovered that he actually enjoyed being trusted to do real work, and spending every day working with his brothers brought them closer together. They formed a newly found fondness for each other, making the work more bearable.

Years went by, and the Mills family fell into a routine; the monotony and lack of change helped them make peace with their life. Despite being a poor family, they were content and made the most of every situation. Joel and his brothers shared a love for singing, possibly a natural talent, and they made quite a name for themselves in the neighborhood. They sang at every event they attended, from singing specials at church to providing entertainment at barn dances; they were always the center of attention. Joel had a wonderful voice and loved the spotlight more than his brothers.

As the years passed, all four brothers, Mark, Josh, Joel, and Bert, went from doing childlike chores such as gathering eggs and growing vegetable gardens to true manual labor like being field hands-on cotton farms and cutting bois d'arc fence posts. With time, all four of them became excellent mechanics and could even build a barn if needed. They continued to sing together, and it brought them joy. Despite the hardships they faced, they found solace and happiness in each other and their music. They enjoyed working together, side by side, and over time, they developed a bond that was unbreakable. They would laugh and joke with each other, and even when things got tough, they knew they could count on each other. Their shared love for the land and their passion for farming brought them even closer together.

It was not always 'all work and no play' for the boys; they made sure to indulge in activities like swimming, hunting, or going to shows on Saturdays. Everything they did, no matter how important or trivial, they always did it together. They were as close as brothers could be until the inevitable happened, and GIRLS GOT INVOLVED! All four boys were strapping lads, they were fairly good-looking, and they knew the kind of effect they had on people, especially girls. They were tall, well-built, and handsome, perhaps because of the physical labor that started very early in their lives, making them appear stronger and more muscular.

However, there was something about Joel that made him stand out to the fairer sex. His dry humor and easy smile had quite an effect on the ladies, and his easy-going personality made girls feel comfortable around him. And so, an upsetting event occurred. The heavens allowed the first girl that kissed Joel to be Angie Rice, the one girl on which his oldest brother, Mark, had a huge crush. As exciting as it was for Joel, it was quite upsetting for Mark. Though when the little romantic kiss happened, Joel had no idea that one of his brothers was head over heels for Angie.

One evening, after Mark found out, he said to Joel, "Why in the hell did you pick her of all the girls at the dance, you little shit!" Joel, at first, did not understand the reason behind his brother's unusual behavior, so he said with a smile, "Hold on, big brother, she asked me to dance, and she asked me to walk with her; I didn't know she wanted to snuggle." Mark was so angry that you could almost see the vein on his forehead popping through his skin, "You should have known I had a crush on her; damn your hide." Joel was not aware of the intensity of Mark's feelings for his crush, so he thought he might as well lighten up the situation with a joke and said, "Shit, Mark, I can't look up your ass and read your mind." Joel, Josh, and Bert started laughing but were instantly interrupted by Mark giving Joel an ass whipping that he was sure to remember for the rest of his life. The incident caused a rift between the brothers, and it took them a long time to heal and mend their relationship.

Mark's physical advantage over Joel was undeniable, and the altercation between the two brothers left a permanent rift in their relationship. As the family sat around the radio listening to the Smoky Mountain blues special, a news bulletin interrupted the program announcing Hitler's military invasion of Poland. France and Great Britain had a treaty with Poland, and the three countries had pledged to defend one another in case of invasion. The family sat in stunned silence, trying to process the gravity of the situation.

The newsman also shared that some politicians raised their concerns about it being a possible start of another world war. As the news continued to play on the radio, Hubert got up and left the house, and no one tried to go after him, perhaps understanding his feelings towards the war. The four brothers knew the location of most of the countries of Europe; they had spent some time looking at the old-world atlas someone had given the family. Although Hubert never mentioned his experience in the first world war, his sons knew he had served in France and had a purple heart in the trunk that held the family photos.

Hubert Mills had seen the horrors of war firsthand. He had fought in the trenches of France, witnessed the death and destruction of war, and carried the physical and emotional scars of it with him for the rest of his life. When he heard about Hitler's invasion of Poland, he couldn't help but feel a sense of dread and despair. He knew all too well the devastation that war could bring, and the thought of his own sons having to go through the same fate was unbearable.

He remembered the look of fear in the eyes of his fellow soldiers, the screams of the wounded and dying, and the smell of death that seemed to linger in the air. He had seen the futility of war and the senseless loss of life. He couldn't shake off the feeling of helplessness and fear. He didn't want his sons to go through the same horrors that he had experienced. He knew that if war broke out, they would be drafted and sent to fight, just like he had been. He couldn't bear the thought of them leaving home as innocent boys and returning as broken men, if they returned at all.

He walked aimlessly, lost in his thoughts, feeling the weight of the past and the fear of the future on his shoulders. He knew that he could not protect his sons from the inevitable, but he could only hope that they would come back home safe and sound. He couldn't shake off the feeling of impending doom, as he knew that the world was on the brink of another devastating war and that his sons would be caught in the middle of it.

Hubert, who had never been a big talker, grew even quieter after the news of the invasion as if drawing an unreachable distance between him and others. He rarely spoke, only answering when asked a question. It seemed to Joel that his father had aged overnight, and his eyes held a dread that couldn't be ignored. The whole family seemed to have a new weight on their shoulders, a burden they could hardly bear. They feared an unknown truth that they knew they would soon discover, and it weighed heavily on their minds.

Chapter 2 - The Storm Is Coming

As the days and weeks passed, the economy began to show signs of life. The government's military spending had started to reach even the most remote corners of the land, bringing a much-needed influx of cash to the rural areas. But despite the financial improvements, there was a sense of unease that hung over everything like a dark cloud. People were on edge, wondering when the next storm would hit. Friends and neighbors seemed to cling to each other, looking for any excuse to come together and enjoy each other's company.

Life went on, but there was a palpable sense of dread that seemed to permeate everything. Joel could feel it too, and it weighed heavily on him. But there was one bright spot in all of this: the local girls. With so much uncertainty in the air, they seemed to be looking for someone to offer them some comfort and affection. And Joel was more than happy to oblige. In fact, he couldn't help but feel a sense of satisfaction in being able to help them, even if it was just a small thing. In a world that seemed to be falling apart, it was something to hold onto.

On that fateful day of December 7th, 1941, the world as the Mills family knew it came crashing down. The surprise attack on Pearl Harbor sent shockwaves throughout the nation and consumed everyone with a deep sense of worry and fear. The lines on the faces of the adults in the family deepened with each passing day as they grappled with the reality of a nation at war. Four months later, Mark, the eldest son of the Mills family, announced that he had enlisted in the Army. Hubert was outraged, and he begged and pleaded with his son not to go, but Mark had already been sworn in, and there was nothing his father could do to change his mind. Over the next few days, everyone in the family found a quiet place to pray for Mark's safety. On the day that Mark was to leave for boot camp, Joel tried his best to give his brother a heartfelt goodbye, but Mark cut him off curtly with a handshake and moved on to the next person. Joel finally accepted that his oldest brother held no regard for him at all.

On September 19th, 1943, the family was celebrating Joel's 18th birthday, but the event was bittersweet. Everyone assumed that Joel would be the third boy from the Mills family to be called to serve in World War II. Josh, the son just older than Joel, had been drafted earlier in the year but was rejected over a bum foot. Just a few weeks before Joel's birthday, they had learned that Mark had been assigned to the US Army postal division and would soon leave for Europe. Even knowing that his job was as safe as any job in a war zone was of little comfort, and the family's fear was overwhelming.

Five long weeks had passed since Joel's birthday celebration, but the memories of cake and presents were quickly overshadowed by the arrival of a letter that would change his life forever. The draft notice, with its stark black letters and official seal, ordered him to report to Lubbock, Texas, for his examination and aptitude testing. The horror of the reality was too overwhelming for the family to bear. As he sat in his room, staring at the notice, a wave of despair washed over him. At one point, his father, Hubert Mills, seriously considered shooting him in the foot as a desperate attempt to keep him from being drafted. He even regretted not doing so immediately.

Joel's mother, a devout holiness woman, couldn't bear the thought of her son going off to war either. Everyone knew that Joel was her favorite, and she knew it was a sin to have a favorite child. But there was something about his quick smile and gentle soul that touched her deeply. She had prayed constantly that they wouldn't take him but had somehow known that they would. Even crusty old Hubert Mills was wracked with worry and fear for his son, as they all knew that this war was not to be taken lightly. The thought of losing him was unbearable, and they all knew that this would be a long and difficult journey for them all.

Joel was a young man of humble beginnings, a hardworking soul who never had quite possessed the raw physical strength or unyielding stamina of his brothers. With his lack of brawn, there was also a certain vulnerability to him that always made Hubert uneasy, tenderness and kindness that seemed ill-suited for the brutal realities of war. As the week before Joel's departure for boot camp at Fort Polk, Louisiana drew to a close; the house was filled with well-wishers, family, and friends, all eager to offer their support and words of encouragement. His favorite uncle, Martin, even made the long journey down from Oklahoma to see him off, bringing with him a bag of ribeye steaks as a rare treat for the Mills family.

As Gladys prepared the feast, the men sat on the porch, smoking cigarettes and looking out over the vast cotton fields that had been the family's livelihood for generations. Martin, a butcher by trade, sat his coffee cup down on the porch and said to Joel, "Son, I hate to see you go, but it's necessary for our country's freedom. I'm sure wherever you go, you'll bring honor to our family and glory to yourself. Hell, I bet you'll come home a hero!"

But Hubert, who had been uncharacteristically quiet up until that point, looked up from the cigarette he was rolling and said in a low growl, "Joel, don't let that bullshit get in your head. There's no glory in war and very little honor, just pain and filth, and suffering. Most of the heroes I've known are rotting in the ground with a stone over their heads, and the world is not one iota better for their deaths. All you need to do is keep your head down and your mouth shut and try to survive. That's the most you can hope for in war." With that being said, Hubert headed to the shed to find his whiskey bottle. He seldom drank, but he sure needed a drink now!

As the men sat in silence, the weight of Hubert's words hung heavy in the air, a sobering reminder of the harsh realities that lay ahead for Joel. But despite the fear and uncertainty that gripped him, Joel knew that he had to go to do his duty and serve his country. And so, with a heavy heart and a fierce determination, he set out to do just that. Hubert's words were harsh but true, and it was clear that he had seen the horrors of war firsthand and didn't want his son to go through the same thing. He couldn't bear the thought of losing another son to this war. Despite the feast, the mood that night was somber and heavy with the weight of war and uncertainty.

It was three days before Joel was to take the bus from Lorenzo to Fort Polk, and he was making the long trek to the small Texas community of Farkle, where the nearest post office was located. He was carrying a long letter to his grandma and grandpa White in Oklahoma, a letter he had been meaning to write for a long time. He missed them dearly and felt a pang of guilt for not having corresponded more. After mailing the letter, Joel went to the small general store and bought a pack of Lucky Strikes and a six-pack of Dr. Pepper, and headed home.

As he walked, his mind was racing with thoughts and memories, a whirlwind of emotions that left him hardly aware of his surroundings. It wasn't until he nearly collided with the old mule pulling Clara Nutall's dilapidated cart that he came back to reality. "Excuse me, Miss Nutall," he said, quickly stepping out of the way. Clara, with a hint of a smile on her face, replied, "Joel, I hear you'll be leaving us soon. I'm sure you have plenty on your mind right now." Joel simply nodded and started to walk away, but Clara stopped him by asking, "Joel, can you spare a few minutes to help me with a task? I'm afraid I can't handle it alone."

Without hesitation, Joel offered his assistance and climbed up onto the cart. Clara explained that she feared the cold of the coming winter and that her bed was too heavy for her to drag inside from her screened porch. She didn't relish the idea of waking up with icicles on her ears, so she asked for Joel's help. Joel, feeling a sense of duty and a deep well of compassion for the woman, agreed to help her. As they rode along in silence, he couldn't help but think about how much life would change for him soon and how much he would miss this small Texas community. But he also knew that it was his duty to serve his country, and he would do it with honor and courage.

As Joel accompanied Clara, his thoughts turned to her. He had seen Clara dozens of times before, always alone in her old cart, but they were far from being friends. He knew she was different, the only woman he knew who lived alone and the only person he knew who raised goats. He knew she made her living by selling goats' milk, candles, and soap she made. As he thought about the task at hand, he couldn't help but be amazed. When they arrived at

Clara's cabin, he opened the screen door for her and was instantly taken back. He had slept on pallets most of his life and couldn't imagine a bed that he couldn't move by himself. Her bed had a massive brass headboard and footboard, the mattress was a foot thick, and it even had metal springs! With some effort, they soon had the huge bed squeezed into the tiny house. They had to push the table and chairs so close to the fireplace that Joel worried they would catch fire.

As Joel turned to leave, Clara's hand reached out and firmly grasped his arm, her touch sending a jolt of electricity through his body. When he looked up at her face, he saw an expression that he couldn't quite comprehend, a mix of sadness and serenity, a beauty that was both haunting and alluring. The look caught him off guard, and he took a step back, unsure of how to react. Clara's hand moved to take his own, her fingers interlocking with his in a soft but powerful gesture. She leaned in close, her breath hot against his ear as she whispered, "Joel, have you ever had a girlfriend?"

He couldn't find the words to respond, so he simply nodded his head, feeling a mix of embarrassment and shame. Clara's eyes locked onto his, a look of longing and yearning that seemed to reach deep into his soul. "Joel," she said, her voice barely above a whisper, "what I'm really asking is, have you ever known the touch of a woman?" The question left Joel speechless, his mind racing as he struggled to find the right words to say, the right way to respond. But in the end, all he could do was stand there, silent and confused, as the moment hung heavy between them. A silent exchange of unspoken longing and desire. Joel couldn't help but feel a sense of sadness for Clara, for the life she had led alone, and for the loneliness that seemed to cling to her like a shroud. He knew at that moment that he would always remember her and the small but powerful connection they had shared.

As Clara gently dropped his hands and stepped back, she began unbuttoning the long row of buttons on the front of her dress. Joel was confused, excited, and nervous all at once, his heart pounding in his chest as he watched her reveal her body, a shapely and beautiful figure that had been hidden under her loose-fitting clothes. He almost turned to run, but Clara gestured for him to come closer, and as she undressed him, she whispered, "Don't worry, Dear, it will be fine; I will help you; it will be fine." And so, she did, and it was.

As Joel made his way home, his mind was awhirl with thoughts and emotions, consumed by the events of the day. The fields, the sky, and the people he passed by were all a blur as his mind was fixed on the memories of Clara. He barely registered his father's voice calling out to him from the field, and at dinner, he ate without truly tasting the food, his mind preoccupied.

As the family moved to the porch, Joel felt a longing to be alone, to process and reflect on what had just happened. He was relieved when his mother and brother went inside to do the dishes, leaving him alone with his father. Hubert's hand reached out, resting gently on his son's arm. When Joel looked up, he saw a rare smile on his father's face, one tinged with a hint of mischief. "Son," Hubert said, "I saw where you came from this evening. Is there anything you want to talk about?" Joel shook his head, unable to find the words, and as his father's smile grew wider, he knew that Hubert understood.

Just as his mom and brother returned to the porch, with a sense of urgency, Joel jumped to his feet and shouted, "Dr. Pepper!" He started toward the road, but the voices of his family behind him, urged him to run until he was out of earshot. As he reached Clara's yard, he hoped for a second that he wouldn't be seen, but her old collie dog started barking, and it seemed like at once Clara was standing on her porch steps. "Joel," she said, "you can come in. Please!" When he left Clara's home for the second time that day, he didn't feel like a scared boy but like a full-grown man. And with that, Joel knew that he would never be the same again.

Chapter 3 - Call of Duty

Finally, the day arrived for Joel to depart for boot camp; in his hand, he carried a small satchel that held his birth certificate, the silver-fronted New Testament his mother had bought him, a few pictures, and his shaving kit. Gladys, Josh, and Bert were ready for the twenty-mile ride to see Joel off at the train depot when Hubert dashed their hopes; he said, "the old bus has a dead battery; I'll have to take him in the pickup." Josh and Bert both said that they would ride in the back of the truck, but their dad rejected their idea because it was too damn cold. Gladys, Joel's mother, pleaded to tag along, but she had been suffering from a cold, and Hubert wouldn't 't take her either. Joel was upset about the situation, but he knew that it would only make her health worse, as a northern had blown in, and it was bitterly cold.

The whole family exchanged hurried farewells that were accompanied by tears. They hugged and kissed him, telling him how proud they were of him and how much they loved him. Gladys cried and hugged him tightly, "Promise me you'll be safe, Joel." Tears rolled from Glady's eyes over her cheeks as her gaze followed Joel as he sat down on the pickup seat.

At that moment, Joel wondered if he would ever see his home again and if he would ever get to work on the farm with his brothers again.

As Joel looked out the windshield, he thought that the steel gray skies perfectly matched the frozen plowed fields as far as his eyes could see. But he kept these thoughts to himself, for he knew that his family was already worried about him, and he didn't want to add to their concerns. The ride continued in silence, the only sound the crunch of the tires on the frozen dirt road. As they headed toward the depot, Joel's nerves began to get the best of him. He had heard stories of the hardships of boot camp and the dangers of war. But he also knew that this was his duty as a patriotic American, and he was determined to serve his country to the best of his ability.

Once the vehicle started and they drove a few miles, he realized that they had nearly reached Clara's cabin. He suddenly wished to see her again one more time, or maybe one last time, as the uncertainty of his life weighed heavy on him. While he was still thinking, his eyes spotted her, and there she was, standing in her yard near the road. She was wearing the same dress as the day before, and she was without a coat or scarf in the freezing drizzle. Joel waved to her as they came closer; she just stood there looking at him with eyes he thought weren't looking at him but through him. A shiver went down his spine, and he turned away.

Hubert broke the silence by asking, "Son, did you know her husband died in the Great War?" Joel didn't respond, and silent tears rolled down both their faces. Joel felt a mix of emotions – fear, excitement, and sadness. But he also felt a sense of purpose, a belief that he was doing something bigger than himself, that he was serving his country and making a difference. The ride was long and uneventful, but for Joel, it was the beginning of a new chapter in his life, a chapter filled with challenges and hardships but also with bravery, camaraderie, and a sense of pride. And despite the uncertainty and fear, Joel was ready to face whatever lay ahead.

When Joel arrived at the boot camp, he was somewhat surprised as he had never been spoken to or even heard the language which the drill sergeants used. But as he got used to the rigorous training and strict regimen, he found that he actually started to enjoy it. The physical activities, the camaraderie, and the diverse range of food were all things that Joel took to. He even began to appreciate parade and drill practice, despite the discomfort of his ill-fitting boots.

With time, he adjusted to his new life and missed home less and less.

Joel's friendly and humorous personality made him popular among the other recruits, and he quickly made a number of friends, including Stacy Phinn, a braggart from Queens, New York. He constantly talked of all the Krauts or Japs he could kill. Not just that, he would say those things with so much certainty that, at times, it made others around him believe that he might even win the war by himself. Despite Phinn's loud and overconfident personality, Joel found something endearing about him, and the two became close. Joel's closest friend at boot camp was Phillip Perdue, a fellow recruit from Louisiana. Both Perdue and Joel came from similar backgrounds, having grown up in poverty and eating similar meals made from wild game and seafood. Perdue even introduced Joel to the delicious crawfish, which he had never tried before.

Joel's training at the boot camp seemed to pass by in a flash, and before he knew it, he was given a 12-hour pass. He and Perdue headed out to a seedy nightclub in Olum. Perdue asked his brother to pick them up. This was Joel's first time in a bar, and he was excited to experience it. He drank too much too quickly and was half drunk when he saw three women enter the bar. They were dressed in skirts that were shorter than anything Joel had ever seen, and their blouses were cut low, showing ample cleavage. To his surprise, he noticed that they weren't wearing bras.

When he pointed them out to Perdue, his friend informed him that they were "camp followers" – women who would sleep with soldiers. "That, my friend, are the women who will screw you for $5.00," said Perdue. Joel was shocked and started to walk toward them; Perdue grabbed his arm and said, Farmboy, I hope you grabbed some rubbers before we left the post; you'll get in a shit load of trouble if you catch something. "Despite the warning, Perdue couldn't help but joke about the situation, telling Joel, "Well, I ain't your momma. Go on, but don't run to me if your pecker is dripping tomorrow."

When he moved close enough to the ladies, he said, "Howdy." The one closest to him, which happened to be by far the ugliest one, grabbed his arm and pulled him outside. As Joel followed her, he was surprised to see the sun was still up. The ugly woman asked, "Farmboy, you looking for some fun?" Without thinking, he pulled out a five-dollar bill and held it out to her. She instantly grabbed it and started to lead him away by his hand; he stopped cold and said, "Ma'am, I was told I would need a rubber." She smiled and said, "Not this time, Romeo." She opened the back door of a brand-new Chevy panel wagon and motioned for him to get in; he was crawling forward when somehow, she rolled him onto his back. He shouted, "Hey." But she had already taken matters into her own hands, and anyone could tell that she was a pro. Joel couldn't believe what she was doing to him; the mastery and precision of it amused him.

As the farm boy who found himself smitten by the allure of camp followers, Joel approached the end of his time in boot camp and artillery school with a mixture of excitement and trepidation. The war games were winding down, and rumors were circulating that they would soon be shipped out to either coast to face the harsh realities of battle. Despite the grim reports coming from both Europe and the Pacific, Joel was determined to do his duty and face whatever lay ahead. He knew he would miss the wild nights spent in the company of the prostitutes, but he was also relieved to leave those dark moments behind, aware of how much it would have shamed his beloved mother if she were to find out.

Joel had struggled with his conscience throughout his time in the army, constantly torn between his love for his family and his own fleshly desires. He had dutifully sent half of his pay to his father, knowing that his family needed the extra income, but often regretting that he couldn't enjoy his newfound freedom and indulge in his vices. He had even considered sending the money to his mother, who worked tirelessly every day without a cent to call her own, but he feared that his father would simply take it from her, given his stingy ways. With a heavy heart, Joel prepared himself for the journey that was soon to come, ready to face whatever lay ahead with the resolve of a true soldier.

Chapter 4 - Over There

The duffle bags of all the soldiers hung heavily over their left shoulders as they awaited their turn to board the cramped train cars. The seats were so close together that one struggled to sit comfortably, while the toilets were nothing more than small wooden barrels placed above a hole in the floor. The thick clouds of cigarette smoke mixed with the heat generated by so many bodies made breathing nearly impossible. It was immediately apparent that the trains were headed west, and rumors spread that their destination was San Diego and a battle with the radical Japanese army led by Hirohito.

The prospect of a three- or four-week voyage across the Pacific, facing a still formidable Japanese navy, was more daunting to the soldiers than the fight against the German army. The train finally started moving, and a loud cheer erupted from the soldiers when they realized it was headed east and not west. Pvt. Stacy Phinn said loudly, "I guess I get to kill that bastard Hitler after all!" The bravado continued to grow as the trains chugged across Louisiana and into the Mississippi delta. The men's spirits were high, with comments ranging from eagerness to get to the war to confidence in defeating the German army.

Men said, "I wish they would hurry the hell up, I don't want to miss the damn war," To, "Hell yeah, we're going to show those Krauts the what Fors," to "Shit man I didn't go through all this training to not get to kill any Nazi bastards!" When the train reached the more populated areas, many of the soldiers were in awe, especially the farm boys and hillbillies from the south and the Appalachians who had never seen such big cities before. Joel awoke from a nap to find himself in New York City, with towering buildings that seemed to reach the sky, and he couldn't help but be in awe.

Suddenly he saw a train disappear under a large building. He turned and said in amusement," Perdue, that damn train went under a skyscraper!" Several men burst out laughing, and one shouted, "Hell, dipshit, haven't you ever heard of the subways?" Joel was terribly embarrassed, but there were so many strange sights no one paid him any attention. Joel and his comrades, along with over 14,730 other soldiers, stood in awe at the New York harbor as they watched countless tanks, trucks, guns, and jeeps being loaded onto ships. The sight of the sheer number of weapons and supplies was overwhelming. The soldiers also caught glimpses of massive cargo nets, filled with unknown goods, being hoisted aboard.

When the soldiers were informed that they would be crossing the Atlantic on the Queen Mary, Perdue and Phinn were ecstatic. Perdue exclaimed in excitement, "Joel, did you hear that, the Queen Mary? We're some lucky bastards!" Joel, who had never heard of the ship, asked in surprise, "What the hell is the Queen Mary?" Phinn, with a hint of disbelief, replied, "Farmboy, I knew you were born in a barn, but I didn't know you lived in it your whole damn life. The Queen Mary is the biggest, most luxurious boat ever made. Kings, queens, and famous movie stars have traveled the damn world on her!" Perdue added, "That's right, my hick friend, I can't wait to see our cabin!" Joel, with a smile on his face, replied, "I've never been on a boat, but I can't wait to see this one!"

The Queen Mary was indeed a marvel of engineering. With its impressive length of 1019 feet, width of 118 feet, and height of 181 feet, it was one of the largest and fastest ships in the world, capable of reaching speeds of up to 32 nautical miles per hour. Despite its grandeur, the ship had been retrofitted for military service and was now painted a dull navy gray. Its beautiful chandeliers, artwork, and other luxurious details had been removed, and the mahogany woodwork was covered in leather. Large barracks had been created by removing walls to accommodate the soldiers, filled with three-tiered bunk beds.

Joel was deeply disappointed by the conditions on the ship. The overpowering smell of diesel, cigarette smoke, and body odor, combined with the constant swaying of the ship, made him and many other soldiers seasick. The humid and stagnant air below deck only made the situation worse. Joel found solace on the deck, where he spent most of his time, even during two days of tumultuous weather.

1.   On the third night of their voyage, Joel stumbled upon a conversation amongst his fellow soldiers about three men who had been caught engaging in a forbidden act. He was puzzled until Phinn enlightened him with a vivid explanation. Though he had read about the matter in the Bible, the reality of it was difficult for him to digest, especially given the nauseous state he was in. The next morning, he overheard Sergeant Humphrey talking about the punishment meted out to the perpetrators. They had been lured to a remote section of the deck under the guise of sharing homemade wine, only to be ambushed by a group of soldiers and tossed into the churning sea.

The incident served as a stark reminder that he was traveling with men far rougher than himself, and he realized he needed to be more resilient if he was to survive.

Finally, on September 14th, 1944, the soldiers disembarked the Queen Mary and began marching towards their new camp. Their destination was Camp McHugh, which was renamed by the GIs as "Fort Blisters" due to the grueling training they underwent. The soldiers were subjected to a twenty-mile forced march; during that forced march, Perdue told Joel, "Our damn brass is afraid we'll never see combat, so they are trying to kill some of us off, so they can fill out some casualty reports." Joel had a good laugh at that thought and said, "If I'm going to die before combat, I would like to get hit by a truck walking back from a bar or whorehouse!" Everyone that heard that statement laughed and agreed wholeheartedly.

During his time in England, Joel was able to forge several meaningful connections with his fellow soldiers. The other NCOs in his company were particularly impressed with his mechanical aptitude and often sought his assistance when it came to repairing equipment. Despite his lack of formal education, Joel also demonstrated exceptional writing skills and was often approached by other soldiers to help compose letters to their loved ones back home. One soldier, a large man from Oklahoma, even noted with a beaming smile, "Old Joel has a real way with words and can spell just about anything you throw at him!"

After five grueling weeks of intense training exercises, Joel and his company were summoned to a large building where they were instructed to write letters to their families. Following this task, they were then given wills to complete and ushered into a mess hall, where they were treated to a delicious meal of chicken and dressing. As a reward for their hard work, each soldier was granted a two-day pass with only a few restrictions. While some chose to rest and recharge in the barracks, Joel, Perdue, and Phinn, amongst others, decided to take advantage of their time off and explore the nearby town.

It wasn't long before Joel, Phinn, and Perdue discovered the potent effects of the dark ale and Scottish whisky they were drinking. Phinn, being his usual boisterous self, nearly got the trio into several scrapes with the locals. Perdue, feeling the weight of the alcohol, declared that he needed some fresh air. Joel and Phinn discussed the situation and decided that they would accompany Perdue back to camp and then make their way back out in search of some female company.

As they were making their way back to base, they were harkened by a middle-aged woman standing in front of a stately, centuries-old home. The three young soldiers approached her with interest, wondering what she could possibly want from them. With a polite smile, the woman said, "We Britons owe you, American lads, a great debt. Would you come in for a nightcap?" Not knowing what a "nightcap" was, Joel replied, "Why, yes, ma'am, we would be delighted to."

Once inside, the woman directed the trio to a warm, inviting room and offered them a nightcap in the form of a generous glass of brandy. Perdue declined the drink, but Phinn eagerly took the offered glass. As Joel settled into the comfortable surroundings, he felt a wave of drowsiness wash over him, but the sip of the strong brandy kept him alert.

The trio expressed their gratitude to the lady, but Perdue then leaned in close to Joel, his voice a hushed whisper. "I think that cursed fish I ate at the tavern was spoiled, Joel. I fear I may retch at any moment." Joel, ever the concerned friend, suggested, "Maybe it's best we get Perdue back to the camp, Phinn. He doesn't look well." Phinn, however, remained unyielding. "Not just yet," he replied matter-of-factly. "If you need to be sick, do it outside, Perdue."

Just as the lady brought them another round of brandy, Perdue suddenly jumped up and vomited on the large coffee table in front of the divan. "My apologies, ma'am," Joel exclaimed. "Allow me to clean this mess." The lady waved away his concerns, saying, "It's quite alright; I'll fetch a damp cloth." As she left the room, Joel turned to Phinn. "By God, Phinn, we need to get him back to camp right fucking now. Look at the poor fellow; he's gone green as the sea." Phinn reluctantly agreed, and as soon as the lady returned with the cloth, they thanked her for her hospitality and started for the door. "Please, stay a little longer," she implored. "My girls will be here soon." Joel regretfully declined, saying, "I'm afraid we must get our friend to camp."

Before the three could reach the street, they were met by four brightly adorned women. Joel immediately recognized them as ladies of the night. The fairest of the four asked, "Where are you gentleman headed so early in the evening?" Phinn began to reply, but Joel interrupted, "Will you be here in the morning? We must attend to our ailing friend and escort him back to camp." The pretty lady replied with a smirk, "Come first light if you like your choices fresh; we stay busy, lads."

When they finally arrived at their barracks, the trio was struck with a severe case of sickness. Perdue proved to be the luckiest of the three, only vomiting once before succumbing to unconsciousness on his cot. Joel and Phinn, however, were not as fortunate. Both were plagued with sickness for hours on end, losing fluids from both ends at an alarming rate. As they huddled together in the lantern light, Joel asked Phinn, "Do you think it was the fish or the oysters that did us in?" Phinn, his eyes filled with anger, snarled, "Why don't you just shut up and leave me the hell alone?"

Despite the situation, Joel couldn't help but laugh. Phinn threw the damp rag he had been using to wipe his face at Joel and stumbled off to bed. As Joel lay down on his cot, he found sleep difficult to come by. Partly due to his upset stomach but mainly due to the guilt and shame he felt at the thought of his mother, Gladys, discovering the debauchery he had partaken in over the past few months. Eventually, his troubled mind gave way to a fitful slumber.

Chapter 5 - First Blood

After a fitful night of troubled sleep, the soldiers were abruptly jolted awake by the echoing cries and the clanging of metal trash cans bouncing against the metal bunk beds. In an instant, Joel was on high alert, his mind still trapped in the rigors of boot camp. Sergeant Blackman bellowed commands, ordering the soldiers to quickly don their uniform and fall into formation outside. There, a stern Major addressed the troops, instructing them to partner up and meticulously inspect their gear. The Major's voice was sharp, brooking no dissent. "Ensure that every single item issued to you is properly secured and accounted for. If any of you funding idiots are missing anything, you had better speak up now, so we can rectify the situation. Because if any of you are short when we get where we're going, you will get the shit kicked out of you, and I'll be the son of a bitch doing the kicking!"

As the morning sun began to climb higher into the sky, the soldiers were mustered out of Camp Blisters for the final time. Each man was shouldered with his own pack, web gear, and an M1 Garand rifle slung over his left shoulder. They were led to a massive assembly point, where Joel was staggered to behold a sea of uniformed men, more than he had ever laid eyes on. It was then that he realized it was the entirety of their division that had gathered here. The clattering of deuce and a half truck could be heard in the distance as platoon after platoon was loaded up and transported away.

By the time Joel's turn came, it was 2 pm, and they were whisked away to a bustling harbor three hours away. There, they were greeted by field kitchens, serving up hot plates of real pork chops and creamy mashed potatoes. Although Joel was starving, he, like many of his fellow soldiers, was too nervous to enjoy the meal. After eating, the men were marched onto the docks, where small ships were departing as swiftly as they could be loaded. Finally, Joel, Perdue, Phinn, and the rest of Company D were ushered aboard, setting sail across the choppy waters of the English Channel, destined for France.

As the small ships approached the coast, the soldiers noticed that there was no apparent shelling, no signs of battle. But as they descended the nets to the landing crafts, their nerves were taut with tension, leaving not one of them capable of breaking wind, not even if it could save their mothers' lives. When the ramps of the landing crafts finally dropped, all the men could see on the beaches were trucks and tanks, an endless parade of machinery. Truck after truck carrying guns and equipment vanished over the hills at the edge of the beach, some requiring tanks to tow them up the steep inclines.

Once ashore, the soldiers were grouped into company-sized formations and marched inland for roughly three miles. There, they were commanded to dig foxholes, establish guards, and then partake of a supper of K rations and coffee. Each man was handed a carton of cigarettes before being ordered to turn in for the night.

The following morning, the three companies that comprised Joel's battalion were loaded into trucks and set off toward the northeast. The half-track leading their truck housed the crew's weapon, the M2 4.2-inch mortar, nicknamed the "goon gun." Weighing in at 333 lbs., this formidable piece of artillery fired 25 lb. shells with a maximum range of 2.7 miles, breaking down into three components: the barrel weighing 105 lbs., the elevation bipod 53 lbs., and the base plate 175 lbs.

Their company commander, Captain Wood, informed them that they were approximately 130 miles from the front, where they would be relieving a brigade that had been in heavy battle for 19 days. After a grueling 4-hour journey in the trucks, the men disembarked and formed ranks. The battalion commander, Colonel Hughes, addressed them, outlining their mission. "We have reports that a small town about 6 miles up the road is occupied by a company of Nazi infantrymen. No artillery has been seen, and it's believed that all French civilians have fled the area. The town is situated in a river basin, with rolling hills on three sides and the river on the far side. We will deploy one company on each of the three sides on this side of the river and use the howitzers to slow their retreat across the two bridges. This is what we've trained for. Let's keep our heads and do what we've been trained to do. Good luck, men; this shouldn't take long." He then turned to the company commanders, instructing them to take control of their men.

An hour later, the infantry was in position, with the howitzers and mortar crews working tirelessly to set up their guns and unload the ammunition. Perdue was to the far left of the village, and Joel and Phinn were setting up to the right. Their crews were two mortars apart. Phinn was helping to unload the heavy base plate when he slipped and dropped it on his left ring finger. It hurt like hell, but he was determined to continue; this day was what he had been waiting for.

When his crew leader, Sgt. Cloudy saw his hand; he immediately told Phinn to hightail it to the aid station and get some stitches put in his hand. Phinn protested loudly until the 2nd Lt. Marsh ordered him to go.

It was at that moment that German shells began to rain down, pounding the trees and surrounding area. The shells sounded like the world was falling apart, and the reality of the situation set in. The Germans were supposed to have no artillery, and the shells were coming from all sides. The battle had begun, and there was no turning back.

As the American troops advanced toward their enemy, their training proved to be a formidable weapon against the Nazis' positions. Joel found himself in the midst of a warzone, with ground and shrapnel flying past him, as the screams of wounded and dying men filled the air. The destruction caused by the American shells was evident as buildings crumbled and burned, leaving the once bustling village in ruins.

Hour after hour, the barrage continued until suddenly, the sound of Nazi guns fell silent. The Americans continued their barrage for a final ten minutes before being ordered to stand down. From his vantage point on the hill, Joel watched in awe as the GI infantry bravely stormed into the town. Afterward, the troops were instructed to clean their weapons, load them on the trucks and conserve the remaining shells.

With their weapons secured, the men began to make their way toward the aftermath of the battle. Joel was accompanied by Perdue as they descended the hill. Upon reaching the ruined streets of the small town, they were confronted with the brutal reality of war. Everywhere they looked, they saw men who had been torn apart by the violence of combat, their limbs and heads missing, their innards spilling grotesquely from their bodies. They were told that nineteen Nazi soldiers had been found dead, with four more badly wounded, but to Joel, it seemed that the number of civilian casualties was much higher.

As they approached a group of infantrymen, Joel noticed that their attention was focused on the ground, and upon getting closer, he saw the small, mangled bodies of three children, their lives cut short, lying on a green wool blanket. The sight was almost too much to bear, and just as he was beginning to process what he was seeing, he saw an older woman carrying another child, this one larger than the others and badly burned from the violence of the battle.

The despair he felt was heartbreaking, and just as he was about to turn away, he overheard one of the young soldiers say, "Jimmy, I can't believe we did this." To which Jimmy replied, "Buddy, we didn't do this; this is artillery. They did this!" The soldier then pointed directly at Joel, with tears streaming down his face. He quickly walked away, unable to bear the weight of the horrors he had just witnessed.

As Joel and Perdue approached their trunks, Martinez, the smart ass from Detroit, summoned them towards him with a wave of his hand. Joel felt an intense dislike towards the large man, his thoughts filled with suspicion over what he could want from them. When they reached Martinez's side, Joel noticed that the sneer, which was usually plastered on his face, was nowhere to be seen. Instead, Martinez appeared to be deeply distressed. Perdue enquired, "What's happened?" Martinez struggled to keep his emotions in check as he responded, "Phinn is gone. He and the bald man from Florida. They were both killed when that shell struck the large tree back there," he gestured towards the aid station.

Martinez turned away, unable to hide the tears streaming down his face. The sight left Joel and Perdue standing in stunned silence. Joel's mind wandered to memories of the good times shared with Phinn, thinking of all the wild things he used to say. In a moment of sudden realization, Perdue grabbed Joel's shoulders and shook him, his voice filled with anger as he exclaimed, "That foolish little son of a bitch, he thought he could single-handedly make a difference and defeat Hitler in this damn war, what a fucking joke. I just want to go home."

With a heavy heart, he climbed into his truck. Joel couldn't help but think about how strange it all was; Phinn had always dreamed of being a hero and had eagerly volunteered to serve, yet he had fallen in the very first minutes of combat, possibly struck down by the first shell that came his way. He had never even had the chance to fire a shot. Perdue's words echoed in Joel's mind; all he wanted was to survive, just as his father had advised.

That night, Joel was thrown back into the chaos of battle as he found himself in the midst of a brutal and bloody struggle near the Hurtgen forest. For the next month, each day seemed to blend into the next as the Americans pushed forward, battering the Germans into submission, only for them to retreat to their next defensible position, where they would dig in and prepare for the next round of fighting.

Chapter 6 - The Bulge

Joel had been hearing the whispers, the rumors circulating among the troops, about the Krauts faltering, about their inevitable surrender. But he knew better than to put his faith in such fanciful notions. In his experience, the enemy was only growing stronger, more resolute, and more ruthless with each passing day. He saw no end in sight. On the fateful morning of December 14th, the battlefield erupted in a deafening roar of explosions and gunfire. Joel was hit, a searing pain tearing through his abdomen as a shard of shrapnel tore through his flesh. He was rushed to a hospital nearly 80 miles behind the front, where a team of skilled surgeons fought to save his life.

For eleven agonizing days, he lay in a hospital bed, drifting in and out of consciousness, his body wracked with pain. The doctors and nurses tended to him with tenderness, but Joel could hardly stand the sight of them. He longed to be back at the front, back with his brothers-in-arms. When the doctor finally gave him the news that he was well enough to return to his unit, Joel was overcome with a sense of relief. He was eager to leave the hospital, eager to leave behind the sterile walls and the incessant moaning of the wounded. He hated doctors and hospitals, and he couldn't wait to put them behind him.

But when he arrived at the front, he was greeted with the crushing news that his company had moved out. He was alone, abandoned, adrift in a sea of chaos and destruction. The next day, he was reassigned to a new infantry brigade and sent out into the fray once again. He marched forward, his heart heavy with a sense of foreboding. He knew that the battle was far from over, that there were still many more battles to be fought and many more lives to be lost. But he pressed on, his eyes fixed on the horizon, his soul hardened by the harsh realities of war.

As they prepared to depart for the Belgium front to the Battle of the Bulge, Joel's thoughts raced with a mixture of excitement and apprehension. He had undergone rigorous training in Louisiana and England, but he couldn't help but feel a twinge of doubt as he lacked infantry experience. Would he have the courage to stand beside the brave men who fought tirelessly in the face of adversity? With a solemn prayer, he hoped he would measure up to the heroes he was about to join in the battle. Upon arrival in France, Joel was already cold, but that discomfort paled in comparison to the icy winds that howled through the Belgian hills as they advanced toward the front. With each step, his heart pounded in his chest as he realized the magnitude of the battle that lay ahead. It was a brutal fight to the death, where the only option was to kill or be killed.

Joel was humbled to fight alongside veterans who had seen the horrors of war firsthand, having fought in North Africa, Italy, and Normandy's bloody beaches. Despite their harrowing experiences, they marched on, determined to push back the German army. The men knew that each inch of territory gained would come at a steep cost, but they persevered through the grueling days and sleepless nights.

The brutality of the battle was unfathomable, with the soldiers constantly at risk of being overrun by the enemy. Their success was measured in hours and yards as they gained and lost ground with each passing moment. In this treacherous environment, Joel found himself tested to his limits, both physically and mentally. As the days wore on, Joel became more than just a soldier; he became a survivor, a hero in his own right. With each passing moment, he and his fellow soldiers forged an unbreakable bond bound together by their shared experience of this hellish battle. And though the horrors of war would stay with them long after they left the battlefield, they knew that the sacrifice they made was not in vain.

The fate of a nation hung in the balance as the Nazis fought with unrelenting fury. Amidst the thunderous explosions and relentless gunfire, Joel witnessed the gruesome aftermath of war. Corpses, frozen stiff with their hands and legs outstretched to the sky, littered the barren landscape. The cacophony of battle was punctuated by the deafening roar of mortars and the wails of the wounded. Joel recoiled in horror as he watched a fellow soldier take a direct hit from a mortar and vanish without a trace, lost to the chaos of war.

Throughout the first week of battle, the elements themselves seemed to conspire against the soldiers. The skies were gray, and snow, sleet, or rain poured down relentlessly. The harsh conditions, coupled with the unrelenting assault of the enemy, took a toll on the morale of the troops. But they pushed on, knowing that their sacrifices were crucial to the war effort.

On the eighth day of nonstop combat, the clouds suddenly broke, and the sun burst through, bringing a momentary respite from the gloom. Soon, the sound of allied bombers and fighters could be heard in the distance, their engines roaring as they swooped down on enemy positions. This was Joel's first experience witnessing aerial raids, and he couldn't help but marvel at the sheer power of the allied forces.

But even as he watched in awe, Joel couldn't help but think of the German soldiers on the receiving end of those bombs. He shuddered at the thought of what they were enduring, trapped in a hellish battle for survival. Yet, even in the midst of such carnage and brutality, Joel and his fellow soldiers never lost sight of the importance of their mission. They fought on, fueled by their unwavering commitment to their country and their fellow soldiers.

The heavy fighting continued unabated, and Joel was desperate for some respite from the relentless onslaught. The screams of the wounded were a constant reminder of the horror that surrounded him, and he wished he could trade places with anyone caught in the crosshairs of a bomber. The sound of human suffering was too much for him to bear. Despite his fears, Joel somehow managed to survive the brutal combat. Then, just as suddenly as the battle had started, the German retreat began in earnest. Joel and his comrades were able to breathe a sigh of relief, but the memories of the carnage they had witnessed would haunt them for the rest of their days.

The next day, Joel and his unit were relieved and sent to the rear for some much-needed rest and recuperation. It was a chance to catch their breath and recover from the physical and emotional trauma they had endured. However, the nightmares that had plagued Joel since the battle only grew worse in the quiet of the camp. Every time he closed his eyes, he saw the gruesome images of soldiers without heads or with entrails hanging out, running towards him in a frenzied panic. He saw the dead children on the green wool blanket and worst of all, he heard the screams of the wounded, piercing his sleep and driving him to the brink of madness. No matter how hard he tried, he couldn't shake the memories of the horrors he had witnessed on the battlefield.

Joel was plagued by another thought, one that had been gnawing at his mind for some time now. He couldn't help but question why he, a mere mortal, was still alive when so many better, braver men lay rotting in the ground. It was a weight that he carried with him, heavy and burdensome, each day feeling like a battle in its own right. The next few months that followed were a blur. Joel merely existed, functioning on unconscious feelings and nervous reactions. The Third

Army was racing across Germany, and while he knew that the war would soon come to an end, he couldn't summon any real sense of happiness. He had been to the depths of hell and back, and the man who returned was not the same as the one who had left.

He found himself wondering if he could ever fit in at home again if he could ever be the man that his loved ones had once known. The very prospect of it was enough to make his blood run cold. And then, on April 13th, 1945, it happened once again. Joel found himself traveling in the back of a deuce and a half truck, slobbering drunk on Schnapps he had taken from a dead SS trooper. The sun was bright, shining down on them as they drove through Allied-held territory on their way to a rest camp. The men around him were singing and joking, their spirits lifted by the knowledge that they were safe at last.

But for Joel, the darkness lingered. He couldn't shake the feeling that he was irreparably broken, that the things he had seen and done had left a stain on his soul that could never be washed away. The idea of going home filled him with a kind of dread that was worse than anything he had experienced in combat. And so, he sat there, trying not to vomit on his boots, lost in a haze of alcohol and regret.

Joel held his head, trying to quell the nausea that was rising in his throat. The truck he was in rumbled along the rough road, jolting its occupants with every bump and dip. Suddenly, without warning, the driver slammed on the brakes, sending all of the men tumbling onto the floor of the truck bed. It was chaos. The Jeep ahead of them had blown a tire, skidding sideways and careening out of control. The soldiers from all three trucks scrambled out, their stiff limbs protesting as they stretched and moved. Joel was the last to leave, crawling down from the truck as the men milled around, trying to assess the damage.

Before they could even begin to make sense of the situation, a shell hit with a deafening explosion. Joel's heart stopped as he watched in horror as both men working on the flat tire were ripped apart, their bodies torn asunder. Shells rained down around them, the ground shaking with each impact. The men ran for cover, their boots pounding on the earth as they sought refuge in a nearby gully. Joel was almost there when he stumbled and fell backward; his body slammed onto the ground. For a moment, he lay there, dazed and disoriented, before he could pick himself up and struggle toward the others. Just as he reached the gully, the truck he had crawled from exploded into a shower of shrapnel and flames.

It was a miracle that any of them had survived. Joel counted the men around him, realizing with a sickening sense of dread that almost half of their small convoy was now gone. But the remaining soldiers held their ground, their trusty M1 Garands at the ready, eyes trained on the wooded hills where the artillery fire was coming from. As the world around them descended into fire and destruction, they stood firm, united in their determination to fight on.

Chapter 7 - Captivity

Part One

None of the American soldiers had any inclination of the danger lurking behind them. They were completely caught off guard when twenty Wehrmacht soldiers, as silent as the grave, crept up to within ten feet of their position. Before they could even begin to react, a commanding German sergeant bellowed orders for them to relinquish their weapons and turn around with their hands on their heads. The Americans, frozen with fear, could do nothing but comply with the demands of their captors.

The only officer present, Captain Castro Wood of Company D, stepped forward to assume responsibility. He offered a formal salute to the Germans, unsure of who was in charge, and spoke with an air of deference, "Sir, you have our surrender, and we will do as ordered." It was a humiliating moment for the Americans, who only moments before had been singing and laughing, blissfully unaware of the peril that lay ahead. They were now prisoners of war on what should have been a bright, sunny morning en route to a rest camp.

Joel, who had been inebriated moments before, was now sober as a judge. He looked around at his fellow soldiers, their heads bowed in defeat, and felt a wave of despair wash over him. The Germans quickly organized the Americans into two columns of four men each and ordered them to move at a double-time pace. The prisoners were forced to jog for close to a mile east of the road they were previously traveling on. The soldiers, once full of vitality and energy, now struggled to keep up with the grueling pace set by their captors. Their hopes of rest and relaxation dashed; they could only wonder what other horrors lay ahead.

When the Germans finally called a halt to the forced march, both the captors and captives were eager to quench their thirst and take a much-needed break. The Germans drank from their canteens and lit cigarettes, and the American prisoners began to do the same. However, Captain Wood intervened, cautioning the men to conserve their water and warning them that the Germans were unlikely to be generous with their supplies. "Men, drink lightly," he advised, "and let's share a smoke. We don't know when we'll get another chance."

As they sat together on the ground, passing a cigarette around, Joel's thoughts turned to the grim fate that awaited them. He couldn't help but recall the tragic fate of the eighty-four Americans executed at Malamy and wondered if they, too, would meet a similar end. But there was little time for reflection as they were soon on their feet again, being herded through the rough, unforgiving terrain. Dense undergrowth, rocky outcroppings, and streams to cross made the journey all the more arduous.

About an hour before sundown, the group marched into a clearing where a camp had been set up. There were only five tents, and Joel could only spot one sentry. The Americans were ordered to sit and wait while the German sergeant ran to the largest tent to report. Within moments an SS major emerged from the tent, accompanied by a small, wiry corporal. The sergeant gave a brief statement before being dismissed by the Major, who then addressed the prisoners.

After speaking briefly with his corporal, the major returned to his tent. The corporal, in turn, sprinted towards another tent and disappeared inside. Moments later, he re-emerged, followed by a tall, handsome SS officer. Joel couldn't help but wonder what was in store for them, but he knew one thing for certain: their fate was now entirely in the hands of their captors.

As the Germans closed in on the prisoners, the little corporal barked out an order, demanding that they stand at attention. Most complied, but the oldest American among them, S.Sgt. McAusland, seemed to pay the order no heed. Suddenly, the sinister-looking NCO whipped out his Luger and fired a single shot, hitting McAusland squarely in the face. The sergeant crumpled to the ground, lifeless, as the other Americans watched in horror.

The tall SS officer, who introduced himself as Dr. Imclind, then began to inspect the captives, scrutinizing them one by one. When he came to Joel, he stopped and asked, "Soldier, will you be able to travel?" Joel, standing stiffly at attention, replied without hesitation, "Yes, sir." But the doctor's gaze fell upon Joel's chest, and he commanded, "Look at yourself." Joel obeyed, glancing down at his blood-soaked field jacket. It was only then that he felt the searing pain in his chin and realized he had a deep gash there. But he did not let his pain show as he met the doctor's gaze and repeated his assurance that he could still travel. The fate of the prisoners now hung in the balance, and Joel knew that he had to stay strong and resolute if he hoped to survive.

The Americans, weary and worn, sat huddled together on the barren ground. The war had taken a toll on their bodies, but their spirits remained unbroken. They watched as the SS troops, their captors, greedily devoured their dinner, a cruel reminder of the deprivation they now faced. Earlier, a German Private had descended upon them like a hawk, snatching their belongings without a second thought. Their web belts, canteens, and cigarettes were all gone, leaving them with nothing but their own wits to survive.

Sgt. Sanchez, a man of few words, finally broke the silence. "I'm not that hungry or thirsty," he said, "but damn man, I could use a smoke." The rest of the men nodded in agreement, the absence of nicotine leaving them on edge. Morning brought no reprieve. They found themselves at the mercy of four SS privates, who spoke in heavily accented English. "Gentlemen," said the one who seemed to be in charge, "my three comrades and I will be taking you to the Province of Susice, where a nice POW camp awaits you. Do know you will be treated well on our journey if you obey all commands. Now let's be on our way."

None of the prisoners, save for Captain Wood, had any inkling of where Susice Province was located.

Wood, a seasoned veteran, knew that they were headed deep into Czechoslovakia. "Men," he said, "I believe the place we are headed is quite a distance away. I have no idea why, so let's all concentrate on getting there alive." The journey was long and grueling. They marched for hours, their stomachs grumbling with hunger. As they watched their captors enjoy a cold lunch and smoke their Camels, the bitterness inside them grew. When night fell, and the SS troops ate yet again without offering them any sustenance, they began to fear the worst. Were they to be starved, left to wither away like discarded refuse?

But they were soldiers trained to endure the harshest of conditions. They steeled themselves against the hunger, clinging to the hope that they would someday be free. They knew that the road ahead would be difficult, but they were determined to see it through. For they were Americans, and they would not be broken so easily.

As the days wore on, the POWs grew increasingly desperate. They had endured hunger, thirst, and endless marches, but their spirits remained intact. On the third day, during lunch, they were pushed to the brink of revolt before the youngest SS guard approached them with a cloth sack. The prisoners eyed him warily, unsure of what to expect. Out of the sack, the guard produced three small balls of burnt bread for each of them. Joel looked down at the pitiful offering with a mixture of disgust and resignation. The bread reminded him of the worst hushpuppies he had ever tasted. He and the other men struggled to swallow the dry, tasteless bread; their throats parched and raw.

Just as they thought they could bear it no longer, the young Nazi noticed their plight and walked over to them, canteen in hand. He tossed it to them, and they scrambled to catch it. The water inside was precious, just enough to keep them alive. They drank greedily, grateful for the reprieve.

This meager ration would be their sustenance for the next twenty days. Three balls of burnt bread once every three days and just enough water to stave off death. They were lucky to be able to drink from the many creeks they crossed, but even that was a gamble. The water was often murky and contaminated, and they risked illness every time they took a sip. On May tenth, 1945, Joel and his comrades were marched into a small POW camp. The sight of other prisoners, mostly pilots from England and Canada, filled them with a sense of relief. They were not alone in their suffering, and perhaps they could find a way to endure it together.

After a meager lunch of broth so thin you could see through it, a group of twelve SS guards sauntered over to the Americans. The guards' demeanor was brusque, and they spoke with clipped cold words. The news they delivered was dire: Hitler had met his end, and Berlin was besieged by the Red Army. They expected the city to fall any day and, with it, the Third Reich. The Americans' ears perked up at this, but the guards weren't finished yet. They leaned in close, their eyes glinting with malice, and revealed their orders to kill all prisoners if Germany surrendered. One guard, towering over the rest, traced his finger across his throat and made a grisly vow to gut the prisoners like pigs.

The threat hung heavy in the air, and the Americans couldn't help but believe every word the guards had said. Captain Wood, in particular, felt the weight of the situation. He sought out the ranking officer among the captives, determined to make a plan of action. Eventually, he found himself face to face with Major Hansel Smith of the Royal Air Force, a round-faced man with rosy cheeks and a pompous air.

Wood relayed the guards' words to the Major, stressing the urgency of the situation. But Smith brushed off the Captain's concerns with a flick of his hand as though he were shooing away a pesky fly. He spouted, "Oh, my dear Captain, you Yanks do love to raise a fuss over nothing! These Germans don't want to kill us; they want assurance they won't land in the paws of the Red Army. So, let's not disturb the subordinates, shall we? We should all stay here and enjoy ourselves until our allied boys retrieve us, I think."

Wood's heart sank at the Major's dismissal of his fears. He knew that if they didn't act fast, they would be sitting ducks waiting to be slaughtered. But he also knew that convincing the Major to take action would be an uphill battle. He steeled himself for the fight ahead, determined to keep his fellow prisoners safe, even if it meant going against the wishes of a superior officer.

Captain Wood's jaw clenched as he took in the pompous dismissal of Major Smith. The man had no grasp of the situation's gravity, and it made Wood's blood boil. He knew that he couldn't sit idly by and wait for the SS to fulfill their blood lust. It was his duty to protect his men, and he would do whatever it took to keep them safe. With a steely resolve, Wood set out to plan their escape. He knew it wouldn't be easy, but he also knew it was their only hope. He gathered his men and explained the situation, asking for their opinions. They all agreed that escape was the only viable option, and Wood was relieved to have their support.

He instructed his men to get as much rest as possible, knowing that they would need all their strength for the ordeal ahead. As the sun began to sink in the sky, Wood summoned his men and revealed his plan. It was a risky venture, but they were all determined to see it through. They would have to move quickly and quietly, staying low to avoid detection. But they were soldiers, trained to adapt and overcome any obstacle. They were ready for whatever lay ahead.

Wood knew that the success of their mission rested on their ability to work together as a team. They would have to trust each other completely, watch each other's backs and cover for one another when necessary. As the night fell around them, Wood and his men set out on their daring escape, their hearts pounding with a mixture of fear and determination. They knew that they were taking their lives into their hands, but they also knew that they had no choice but to try. And so, with a fierce determination burning in their hearts, they slipped into the darkness and disappeared into the night.

The men gathered in quiet apprehension as they awaited their next mission. Their exhaustion was showing, weighing down on them like a heavy yoke. But despite their fatigue, sleep evaded them, and they lay in restless silence. As the sun began its descent, the Captain roused his men from their slumber, determined to maximize their rest before the task at hand. In a low voice, he outlined his plan to the group. Joel and Pvt. Snow would take down the two guards that patrolled the nearby area, using whatever means necessary. Then, they would break into the nearby tool shed and retrieve wire cutters to access the fence.

At the mention of his name, Joel's heart skipped a beat. The responsibility placed upon him was immense; Joel asked, "Sir, did you say me?" Captain Wood answered, "Yes, you and Pvt. Snow are the youngest and largest of us. Is there a problem?" Joel quickly said, "Oh, no, sir, I just didn't hear you well." The men quickly set to work, tearing apart a wooden bed in the corner of their assigned building to use as makeshift weapons. The plan hinged on the predictability of the SS guards. They knew the guards' routine, knew that they would meet at the center point of their patrol, smoke and converse for a brief time, then part ways.

Joel and Snow were to wait on opposite ends of the building, ready to strike, when the guards walked past. The tension among the men was overwhelming as they waited, their hearts pounding in their chests, adrenaline coursing through their veins. They knew that their success would mean the difference between life and death for them and their comrades. And so, they waited with bated breath for the moment to strike.

Joel's heart was pounding in his chest as he crouched in the shadows, his eyes fixed on the SS guard, who was slowly making his way toward him. It was a simple plan, but Joel knew that one false move could mean certain death for himself and his fellow Americans. He watched intently as Snow, his comrade-in-arms, waited patiently for the right moment to strike.

The German guards had been smoking and laughing for what felt like an eternity, but finally, the moment had arrived. Snow made his move, and Joel sprang into action, his muscles tense and ready for the fight ahead. His heart racing, he charged toward the SS guard, his fists holding his club tightly. The guard spun around on his heels, but it was too late. Joel's thundering blow landed squarely on his forehead, and the guard crumpled to the ground, unconscious.

Adrenaline surged through Joel's veins as he rained blow after blow on the fallen German. He had never been in such close combat before, but he was a soldier. It was only the firm grip of Captain Wood on his arm that brought him back to reality. With a start, Joel looked around, taking in the scene before him.

The Americans were all there, kneeling by the fence, their faces grim as they worked to cut through the barbed wire. Joel felt a surge of relief wash over him as he realized that they had all made it through the dangerous first step unscathed. But the mission wasn't over yet. They had to get out of there and fast.

"Let's get the hell outta here!" Captain Wood's voice cut through the tense silence, and Joel turned to follow him, his heart still pounding in his chest. As they made their way towards the fence, Joel glanced back at the fallen guard, his mind filled with conflicting emotions. He knew that what they had done was necessary, but he couldn't help but feel a sense of guilt and remorse for what he had done.

It seemed as if they were making progress, with only one or two wires left to cut, when the sound of rifle fire shattered the night. Snow didn't hesitate, diving through the hole in the fence with the rest of the group close behind. But as they ran, they heard a sickening thud and a low groan and turned to see Snow lying face down on the ground. Half of his face was gone, including his left eye, and there was no doubt that he was dead.

The Captain dropped down beside Snow and turned him over, his face filled with grief and anger. He paused for a moment, his eyes fixed on the fallen soldier before rising to his feet and shouting, "Run, damn it, run!" And so they ran, their hearts heavy with sorrow and fear, but their legs carrying them forward through the darkness.

They ran through muddy fields, their boots sinking into the muck with every step. They pushed through briar patches, feeling the sharp thorns tear at their skin. They waded across creeks, the icy water biting at their legs, and stumbled over sharp rocks, their muscles aching with exhaustion. But they kept going, driven by a fierce determination to survive.

They had no way of knowing how far or how long they ran. Time seemed to stretch out endlessly before them, each step becoming harder and harder to take. They were wading uphill in a small creek, their bodies battered and bruised, their clothes torn and bloodied. Every breath was a struggle, every movement a triumph over pain and exhaustion.

But they kept going, driven by a deep-seated sense of duty and loyalty to their fallen comrade. They knew that they couldn't stop, couldn't give up. They had to keep running and keep pushing forward, no matter what the cost. For Snow, for themselves, for all those who had fallen before them.

Captain Wood halted his men and surveyed the treacherous terrain ahead of them. The steep banks of the little creek they were approaching looked like they were practically vertical, and the surrounding landscape provided no cover to shield them from enemy fire. The Captain took a deep breath and turned to his exhausted troops.

"Listen up, boys," he said. "We gotta make it to the top of that hill, and we gotta do it fast. Once we get up there, we'll hunker down and take shifts resting. With luck, we can stay hidden until tomorrow night, so keep your eyes peeled and your wits about you."

The men nodded in silent agreement, steeling themselves for the arduous climb ahead. But as they crested the hill, they were greeted not by a respite but by the cold metal barrels of three rifles trained on their heads. A woman's voice rang out, commanding and unyielding. "Climb on out, hit your knees, then put your hands on your head."

The men obeyed, their hearts racing with fear and uncertainty. Captain Wood, ever the leader, spoke up in a calm, measured voice. "We are Americans, 3rd Army, 179th Infantry. We just escaped from the prison camp at Susice." A man with broken English stepped forward, his face a mask of suspicion and mistrust. "Stand up," he ordered.

As the men rose to their feet, two women moved in to search them for weapons. Finding none, the man shone a small flashlight at Captain Wood, examining him closely. The Captain's once-pristine uniform was now torn and tattered, his face and hands caked with dirt and grime from weeks of captivity. "Tell me the story of how you came here," the man demanded.

Captain Wood took a deep breath, gathering his thoughts. He knew that their survival depended on the goodwill of these strangers, and he would have to convince them that they were on the same side. "I'll tell you anything you want to know," he said. "But first, can you feed my men? They're starving."

The man hesitated for a moment before nodding his assent. He motioned for the women to lead the Americans to a nearby campfire as Captain Wood recounted their harrowing journey from the prison camp, detailing their daring escape and the dangers they had faced along the way.

Joel and the other bedraggled men stumbled after their captors, their muscles aching and their spirits low. The rain continued to pour down on them, drenching them to the bone and sapping what little energy they had left. But as they approached the freedom fighter's cave
they saw a flicker of light in the darkness that gave them hope.

One of the women tended to the campfire, adding more wood until it blazed bright and hot. The Americans crowded around it, grateful for the warmth and light that it provided. Joel couldn't help but notice the contrast between the cold, wet darkness outside and the warm, inviting glow of the fire. The women soon returned with heaping plates of food, each one piled high with a variety of sustenance. There were slices of dark rye bread, boiled mussel shells, tangy sauerkraut, and sharp, pungent cheese. The aroma of the food was enough to make Joel's stomach growl with hunger. The women also brought tin cans filled with strong coffee, which the men eagerly gulped down.

Joel took a cube of sugar offered by one of the women, savoring the sweet taste on his tongue. He was about to accept another when he heard a giggle. Looking up, he saw both women smiling at him, their eyes sparkling with amusement. He quickly refused, not wanting to appear greedy or ungrateful. Captain Wood appeared, barking orders to the men. "Get some rest," he said. "Sgt Sanchez, make a roster for guard detail."

But before Sanchez could respond, one of the women spoke up. "Captain, we have been fighting the stinking Nazi for almost four years," she said. "I think I can protect my camp one more night." Captain Wood nodded, impressed by her spirit and determination. "Very well," he said. "Men hit the sack."

Joel and the others settled down for the night, the warmth of the fire and the comfort of a full stomach providing a small measure of solace in the midst of the chaos and uncertainty of war.

Joel woke up from a deep slumber, feeling the warmth of the campfire still lingering on his skin. He winced as he touched the wound on his chin, which had become infected and was now oozing pus. The smell was nauseating, and the discharge had made his beard sticky and wet. But despite the pain, he felt rested for the first time in weeks.

Captain Wood woke the rest of the men, announcing that breakfast was ready and that they needed to talk about their plans for the day. It was still dark outside, and Private Hedman checked his pocket watch to find that it was only 2:30 in the morning. The men were grateful for the warm meal of bread, cheese, and fresh goat's milk, and several pots of coffee helped to bring them back to life.

As Captain Wood approached, Sgt. Sanchez asked about the nearest troops and the likelihood of finding them. Instead of answering, Captain Wood came to a halt and snapped, "Fall in!" The six men jumped to their feet and stood at attention. This was the first time he had done this since the day of their capture. He looked closely at his men and said, "We won't be looking for the allied lines today. We will join the freedom fighters under the command of Mr. Jelandski and march back to Susice and liberate the remaining prisoners there. The commander and I believe this is the only choice to ensure the safety of our allies there. We will accomplish this by disarming the four sentries; then, we will capture the Commandant and demand the surrender of the rest of the guards. We will move out at four am. Have some more coffee, and the women will be boiling a large pot of water; if any of you would like to clean up some. Joel, have someone help you clean your wound before it gets any more infected. At ease."

He turned on his heels and made his way back towards Mr. Jelandski, the commanding officer of their small band of fighters. Joel couldn't help but wonder if the man had ever slept. He hadn't caught a glimpse of the Captain resting in days, nor had he seen him consume a single morsel of the meager rations they had been provided. Most officers were held in contempt by the enlisted men, and Joel was no exception, but Captain Castro Wood had managed to earn his unyielding respect and admiration.

As they waited for their next mission, the two women appeared with scraps of cloth fashioned into makeshift washrags. They introduced themselves as Selba Plansky and Matka Zelandsky, the commander's wife. Both women were Polish and had fought valiantly against the Nazi invasion until the price on their heads had become too high. They then fled to Czechoslovakia to continue their battle for freedom.

After introductions were made, the men gathered around a large pot of boiling water for a much-needed wash. Selba noticed the deep gash on Joel's chin and offered to tend to it. He winced as she tried to clean the wound, but he appreciated her gentle touch nonetheless. She took a small pair of scissors and carefully trimmed the jagged edges as best she could. Once she finished, they joined the others by the campfire.

Joel poured himself a can of coffee and sat down next to the other men. As they sipped their bitter brew, they talked about their loved ones back home and the dreams they hoped to realize once the war was over. It was a small moment of respite in the midst of the confusion and bloodshed, but it was a moment that Joel would always cherish.

Part Two

Soon, Selba moved in front of them and said, "Men, here is our plan of attack and assigned duties; we will arrive at Susice before sunrise. We know there is a door on each side of the barracks. We also believe each door will have one sentry posted there. We will be in two-person teams." Then she took a stick and drew a rectangle in the dirt. She pointed to the right side of her drawing and said, "Matka and I will have the side closest to town, Sgt. Sanchez and Pvt. Hedman will have the front of the building, Pfc. Tracy and Pfc. McCall will take the left side, And the two Corporals will take the rear," she said, pointing at Joel and Corporal Brian Klinks.

"Each team will secure cover as close to their door as is safe. Our signal to move in will be your Captain honking a truck horn one time. We will then charge our positions, with no gunfire, if it can be avoided. We will disarm the sentries, and I will then come around the building and take the prisoners to a place designated by our leaders. There I will watch three German prisoners, and the fourth will be forced to lead the officers to the Commandant's quarters. Captain Wood will alert you as to when to make entry into the barracks. With luck, The Commandant will order the remaining Germans to surrender. Any Questions?" Pvt. Tracy piped in and said, "Yeah, why are we getting orders from a damn woman instead of the Captain?" Immediately Sgt. Sanchez backhanded Tracy to the ground and said, "Dumb ass, these women have seen more action than you ever will so shut the fuck up and do as you're told!"

The order was given, and the men stood at attention, clutching the old Mauser rifles they had been handed. Joel and his comrades wished they had better weapons, knowing that the stakes were high and any mistake could cost them their lives. One of the men had managed to obtain a SS guard's rifle during their daring escape the night before, but the group feared the potential consequences of being caught with such a weapon.

As they crept towards Susice, the darkness enveloped them, but they knew they had been spotted by at least two people. Zelandsky reassured them that the Czechs despised the SS even more than they did, offering some comfort to the anxious soldiers. The barracks loomed ahead, an old hotel that had been repurposed for the SS. It had four doors, just as the Poles had reported.

Captain Wood addressed the team, rallying their spirits and reminding them of the noble cause for which they were fighting. They were to free the prisoners and bring them home, an act that would be a source of pride for all involved. The men split into four teams and quickly found cover, waiting for their moment to strike.

Joel's heart pounded as the sound of the horn signaled the beginning of the attack. The next ten seconds seemed to stretch on forever as the teams rushed toward the SS guards, meeting little resistance. With swift and determined action, they overpowered the enemy, taking their coveted SS daggers as spoils of war. The captured guards were marched away, and the teams regrouped, preparing for the next phase of the mission.

Captain Wood carefully assigned each team member to their role, ensuring that the prisoners would be freed with minimal risk to anyone's life. One person would enter the barracks on each side while the other guarded the outside, watching for any signs of danger. With a stern warning, he added, "no gunfire unless it's life or death!" the soldiers prepared to make their move.

As the captured guard led Captain Wood and the Zelandskys through the barracks, Joel's fellow companion Matka, stood guard outside the door, her eyes scanning the surroundings for any potential threats. The fate of the mission hung in the balance, but the bravery and determination of these soldiers would not falter. They were fighting for a noble cause, one that would make a difference in the lives of many.

The Commandant, Major Guunt, stood before his mirror, razor in hand, as the three men barged into his quarters. He raised his eyes to meet their gaze and continued shaving, taking his time with each stroke. With a final rinse of his face, he reached for his shirt and methodically buttoned it up. When he was ready, he marched up to Captain Wood, saluted him, and introduced himself as the Commanding Officer. But before he could get another word in, Mr. Zelandsky interjected, informing the Major that he was now a prisoner.

The Major remained at attention, his eyes fixed on Captain Wood. He said, "Captain, is this what you would have me do?" Captain Wood confirmed that it was and reminded him that he was to obey Commander Zelandsky's orders just as he would his own.

The Major's lips curled into a smirk, and he responded with a sinister tone, "Captain, that won't be happening today." And with that, he strode into the hallway, his voice booming with authority. "This is Major Guunt; we have been overrun by American forces. I order each of you to come out of your rooms unarmed, with your hands on your head. There will be no more bloodshed!"

The Major's heart raced as he awaited the response of his men. He hoped they would heed his call and surrender without a fight. As he stood there, he couldn't help but feel a pang of regret for the chaos and destruction that had brought them to this moment. But he knew that he had to do what he could to end this without bloodshed and get his men safely into the hands of the American army.

The SS guards stumbled out of their rooms, still bleary-eyed and half-dressed, their hands raised in surrender. But as they shuffled into the hallway, two of their comrades burst out from a side room, firing their Lugers wildly. Matka reacted with lightning speed, taking down the rogue soldiers before they could do any more damage. But the carnage had already been wrought, with two of their own dead and another gravely injured.

The Americans quickly rounded up the surviving Germans, forcing them to sit outside with their hands on their heads. They scoured the building for any usable weapons, and as they did, they each snagged a souvenir or two. With the prisoners secured, the three Polish fighters volunteered to keep watch while Captain Wood and his men went to liberate the POW camp. They were led by Major Guunt, who stood tall and proud with his blond-haired orderly by his side. As they approached the camp's front gate, the Major bellowed his orders, his voice carrying the weight of command.

The orderly unlocked the gate and, without hesitation, ran into the camp to deliver the Major's message. Soon, a group of guards appeared on the right side of the camp, followed by three more from the left, their rifles at the ready. The Americans wasted no time, taking down the rogue soldiers before they could cause any trouble.

The remaining guards were left with no choice but to surrender, holding their rifles high above their heads as they made their way through the gate. Major Guunt then shouted, "Men, no more foolishness. Would you rather fight today and be Russian prisoners tomorrow?" And with that, they meekly submitted to their American captors.

As soon as the last of the prisoners had been searched and secured, Captain Wood marched into the camp; his jaw set firm with determination. His eyes scanned the area, searching for the pompous English Major who had been causing so much trouble. Spotting him lounging under a tree, Wood strode over, his boots thudding on the dirt. He approached the Major and stood before him, his voice clipped and precise. "Major Smith," he said, "I need to know if you and your men are ready to travel."

The Major sneered, his lip curling in contempt. "Silly Captain," he replied, "most of my men are too sick or fragile to march. But I have a plan. Give me rifles and ammunition, and I will arm the able-bodied men and set up a perimeter guard. We'll hold out until you return with trucks to get us out of this God-forsaken place. And Captain," he added with a mocking grin, "don't forget to send a jeep for me. I wouldn't want to ride in the back of a bloody truck."

Wood gritted his teeth, his patience wearing thin. But he kept his voice even as he replied, "Anything you wish, Major." With a curt nod, he turned and walked away, eager to be rid of the arrogant fool. As he made his way back to the front of the barracks, he saw that Matka and Selba had the prisoners in formation, ready for the Americans' return. Commander Zelandski approached him, his face grave with concern. "Captain," he said, "I don't know how the townspeople will react when they see the Germans. But I swear to you, I will not let myself or my women be harmed. Do we have an understanding?"

Wood nodded, his eyes blazing with determination. "Absolutely," he replied. "I'll speak to my men and make sure they understand. We won't let any harm come to your people."

With a crisp salute, he turned back to the formation, his heart heavy with the weight of responsibility. War was a brutal, unforgiving business, and he knew that every decision he made could mean the difference between life and death for his men, the prisoners, and the innocent civilians caught in the crossfire. But he was a soldier, and he would do his duty to the best of his ability, no matter the cost.

Amidst the sea of captured Germans, several of them spoke English, their faces etched with fear and desperation. One of them, standing near Joel, spoke up. "Hey," he said, his voice tinged with hope, "we were glad you GIs showed up. We knew the war was lost, and we damn sure didn't want to end up being taken by the bastards of the Red Army; they're nothing but barbarians. I hope I get to go to America; I have family there. Do you think I will make it to the USA?"

Joel looked at the SS henchman with cold fury. How could he be so naive, so blind to the atrocities committed by his own kind? "How can you think you are any better than the Russians?" he spat. "You rape and torture and kill for fun. I don't give a damn what happens to you, but I would bet you see a firing squad before you see America."

Captain Wood waved for his men to join him away from the prisoners, his face set in grim determination. "Zelandski thinks the townspeople may make a grab for the Germans," he said. "We will take positions at the rear of the formation; if the Czechs do attack, we will fall back and observe. I won't allow any of you to die protecting these SS sons of bitches. Are we clear? Let's get started; I'm ready to find our army and have some good old American food!"

The men chuckled at Wood's words, their laughter easing the tense situation. They took their positions, their rifles at the ready, as Selba led the formation toward town. As they approached, Joel could see that the Germans were marching with a false bravado, their heads held high as if they were in a parade in Berlin. The street was lined with people on both sides, old men, children, and women of all ages. But there were no younger men or teenage boys; they had either been killed, conscripted, or were hiding in the forest with the Czech freedom fighters.

Joel felt a sickening sense of anger and sadness at the sight of the civilians. They had suffered so much under the Nazi occupation, and yet the Germans marched through their town as if they owned it. He knew that the situation was volatile, that one false move could set off a powder keg of violence. But he was a soldier, and he would do his duty to protect his comrades and the innocent people caught in the crossfire. The war had taught him that life was fragile and fleeting and that the only thing that mattered was to stay alive and fight for what was right. And so he marched on, his heart heavy with the weight of responsibility, his eyes scanning the crowd for any signs of danger.

As they approached, a bloodthirsty crowd gathered in the town square, their fury fueled by a burning desire for revenge. The SS guards, feared and loathed, had finally met their match. The townspeople had armed themselves with whatever makeshift weapons they could find and unleashed their fury upon the hated enemy. The sounds of hammers, axes, and knives striking flesh echoed through the streets as the mob dragged the SS guards around, stabbing and beating them mercilessly. The air was thick with the scent of blood and sweat, and the ground was slick with the gore of fallen foes.

As the violence subsided, the townspeople began to strip the SS guards of their uniforms and dignity, hanging their lifeless bodies from the telegraph poles that lined the streets. But one man, the Commandant, remained untouched, his courage and arrogance defiantly on display. Joel, a soldier hardened by the horrors of war, admired the Major's bravery, even as he despised his affiliation with the SS.

Suddenly, two old men appeared, leading two small donkeys wearing harnesses. They positioned the animals on either side of the Commandant and wrapped chains around his arms and legs, hooking them onto the donkey's harnesses. Joel watched in fascination, wondering what the small animals could do. But as the donkeys were slapped and prodded forward, Joel soon found out. The Major remained silent even as the donkeys pulled him apart, screaming a final, blood-curdling cry of allegiance to Hitler.

In the aftermath of the carnage, Zelandski approached the Americans and offered his help at the POW camp in exchange for weapons and ammunition. The Americans had grown fond of their Polish comrades and were sad to part ways, but they had a mission to complete, and with handshakes and hugs, they headed west in search of Allied troops, leaving the town and its gruesome memories behind.

Word had spread that the Americans were closing in, and the group was eager to make their way to safety. As they neared the edge of town, a sudden commotion startled them. A group of women, their faces lit up with joy, were running towards them. The men recoiled in fear, haunted by the memory of the brutal mob they had encountered earlier. But to their surprise, the women showered them with hugs and kisses and gifted them a wicker basket overflowing with food. Bread, cheese, jam, wine, sardines, and honey - it was a feast fit for kings. The men were grateful for the sustenance, but their weakened bodies could not handle such a sudden influx of nourishment. They gorged themselves until their stomachs were tight with discomfort.

Joel's fever was raging, his head pounding, and his vision blurred. The others were struggling, too, their bodies pushed to the brink of exhaustion. They trudged on; the once-paved highway was now reduced to a rugged wagon track, overgrown with trees and foliage. Sanchez noticed Joel's condition worsening and suggested they rest for a while. Captain Wood agreed, "Yeah, let's take ten." and the group stopped for a much-needed rest.

Joel sat down, his body aching and his mind heavy with worry. Would they make it to safety? Were US forces truly just a few miles away as they had been told? He longed for relief, for the end of this endless march through hostile territory. The men sat in silence, each lost in their own thoughts, their fate uncertain.

As they lay to rest, the soldiers caught sight of movement in the thick foliage on either side of the road. Then soldiers emerged, guns drawn, and orders were barked to the weary American ex-prisoners. Joel's heart leaped with hope as he recognized the uniforms of his fellow countrymen, but his body had reached its limits, and he collapsed onto the dirt, his face smacking against the ground.

After interrogating the ragged group, SSgt. Corn confirmed their identities and radioed for backup. The exhausted soldiers were finally able to let their guard down and fell into a deep slumber, their weapons within arm's reach. Joel's fever had reached a dangerous level, and he drifted in and out of consciousness. His mind was hazy, and his body felt weightless, as though he were adrift on a turbulent sea. Waves of nausea overtook him, and he longed for the comfort of a good night's sleep.

As he roused from a fitful nap, Joel caught sight of his fellow soldiers stretching their aching bodies. He noticed Captain Wood deep in conversation with a Lieutenant from the Twentieth Corps, Third Army.

Joel had begun to believe that the Captain was not a mere mortal but a machine wrapped in flesh. He never seemed to tire, ate sparingly, and appeared to never sleep. As Joel's respect for the man grew, he couldn't help but wonder if the Captain had left his humanity behind somewhere in the chaos of war. The fifteen-mile Jeep ride was a torturous journey for Joel, each bump sending a wave of pain through his head. He had endured a horrific last month as a prisoner of war, and the thought of dying before reuniting with American troops weighed heavily on him. He hoped to last long enough to write a letter home, to ease his parents' worry, knowing they must be consumed by fear.

The Jeeps arrived at a camp and parked in front of three large tents. The corporal driving the lead Jeep rushed into the largest tent. Captain Wood and his ragged troops crawled out of the cramped Jeeps and stood in the road, greeted by a large group of fresh-faced soldiers in crisp uniforms. The new replacements noticed the exhausted escapees and rushed over with two long wooden benches. Everyone sat down except Captain Wood, who remained standing, a picture of military discipline.

Soon after, the corporal emerged from the tent, followed by several officers led by a Colonel. Captain Wood called his men to attention, and the Colonel ordered them to sit. As he approached, Captain Wood gave him a sharp salute, which the Colonel returned, then ordered him to stand at ease. The old officer requested Captain Wood's account of their ordeal, and the Captain gave a brief overview, from their capture to the Czechoslovakian's brave attack on the SS guards. As he recounted their harrowing story, everyone noticed the Captain began to tremble.

The Colonel interrupted, "That's enough for now," and reached out to shake the Captain's hand. As they clasped hands, Captain Wood's knees gave way, and the Colonel helped him to the ground. He called for a stretcher, and the exhausted officer was carried away, his body broken by the physical and emotional toll of the last month. The men watched in silence, grateful for the Captain's unwavering leadership and courage and deeply aware of what it had cost him for their survival.

Joel and the other escaped prisoners of war were ushered into a nearby tent, where they found cots awaiting them. They were so exhausted that they barely registered the arrival of food and coffee before they fell into a deep sleep. The next morning, they were awakened by Pvt. Marks, who had been assigned to guide them. He greeted them with an overzealous statement about heroism, which fell flat among the tired and battle-weary men. He quickly changed the subject to breakfast.

After breakfast, Marks led the men to the showers, where they gratefully rid themselves of weeks' worth of grime and filth. Marks handed each of them a small wooden ammo box and instructed them to place their personal belongings inside. He promised to dispose of their filthy uniforms and provide them with new ones. As Joel rummaged through his pockets, he discovered a handful of German coins, his wallet, and a book of postage stamps featuring Hitler on the cover. He tossed his field jacket to the ground and then retrieved a silver-plated New Testament from his left shirt pocket.

As he was about to drop it into the box, he noticed something strange. A hole had been punched through the cover, and it was clear that a bullet or shrapnel had passed through it, exiting straight through the top. Joel realized that the object in his hands was the very Bible that had saved his life. He called out to the others, holding it up for them to see. "Hey, fellows, take a look at this shit," holding the small Bible out. They all came over and looked closely at it. Pvt. Hedman said, "My gosh, Joel, it's a miracle you're alive! That Bible saved your life."

The men gathered around him, marveling at the bullet hole and expressing their astonishment that Joel had survived. Pvt. Hedman declared it a miracle, and Joel couldn't help but agree. The Bible had become a talisman of sorts, a reminder of the danger they had faced and the luck that had kept them alive.

Joel's heart sank as he realized the others were now treating him like a saint, thanks to the bullet-riddled Bible that had saved his life. He wished he had kept quiet about it, knowing that the story would follow him around like a bad smell. As they moved on to the showers, Joel couldn't help but feel a sense of relief. The water was hot and soothing, and it felt like a luxury compared to the past month spent in captivity. They all scrubbed themselves raw, trying to rid their skin of the grime and filth that had accumulated during their imprisonment. Joel couldn't help but agree with Pvt. McCall's assessment that the shower was better than sex. The laughter that followed was a welcome sound after the horrors they had endured.

As they stepped out of the showers, they were handed fresh uniforms and hospital slippers. Joel felt a sense of relief as he slipped into the clean clothes, feeling like a new man. His feet were in terrible shape from the long march, and the blisters made walking excruciatingly painful. He was grateful for the slippers that would give his feet a much-needed break. The men were beginning to look like soldiers again rather than emaciated, beaten-down prisoners. Joel felt a flicker of hope in his heart, knowing that they were on the road to recovery.

The convoy soon pulled into a makeshift barber tent, and Joel and his comrades had their heads and faces shaved. Lice solution was applied to their bug-bitten skin. Joel winced as the razor scraped his skin, and he feared he might pass out from the pain. Once they had been primped and cleaned, the group was driven to the hospital tent. When the doctor took one look at Joel's face, he said, "My Lord boy, why didn't you come here last night? Are you trying to lose half your face!" Without waiting for an answer, he called, "Orderly, clean this wound, then take this boy to see Dr. Wallace." The orderly showed no mercy; he scrubbed and squeezed Joel's chin until tears ran down his face. When he finished, he took Joel by the arm and led him to a small tent a few yards away. Joel sat on a metal chair and waited.

When the doctor showed up, he said, "I'm Dr. Wallace; let's have a look." he took hold of Joel's chin and slowly moved it one way, then another. Then he said, "Young man, this is more than I can stitch; we will treat you here until we get this infection under control; then I will send you to Paris to have a skin graft done." Joel quickly replied, "Sir, is that really necessary? I want to rejoin my unit as soon as possible." The doctor looked amazed and said, "Where have you been, son? You won't be going to the line; the damn Germans surrendered this morning! You'll be going home." Joel was stunned by the news and very relieved. But he found himself thinking of his friends and all the good men he had seen die or injured. He just couldn't make himself feel happy, not yet.

A few mornings after Joel's ordeal, a newly-promoted Major Wood entered the dimly lit tent where the men were staying. It took Joel a moment to recognize that the man he had known as Captain Wood was now a Major. The men greeted him with handshakes and pats on the back as he made his way through the tent. Major Wood announced that he would soon be transferred to Nuremberg to help capture and prosecute Nazi war criminals. The men engaged in small talk for a while before Major Wood mentioned that he had a staff meeting to attend and would see them at the upcoming medal ceremony.

As he was leaving, he paused and pulled a folded paper out of his pocket, "Guys, I took this out of Snow's pocket the night he was killed. I assumed it was a letter home, but it's not. I'm afraid it might upset his parent, but I thought you might want to read it." McCall took the paper and read it, his face turning pale. When Hedman asked him what it said, McCall didn't respond and simply passed the paper to the next man before leaving the tent. Joel, who happened to be the nearest, read the paper to himself and heard the other men asking what it was about. He knew three of them couldn't read, so he read it in a low voice, "My Buddies," Troubled times, Troubled places. The distant stare on troubled faces. They've sailed, they've marched. They've swum, they've crawled. They did their best; they gave their all. I've watched them win; I've watched them try. But most of all, I've watched them die." Andrew Snow.

Chapter 8 - Coming Home

Part One

On that somber August day in Felsberg, Germany, Joel cast his gaze upon the solemn visages of his comrades. The lines etched upon their faces told tales of horror and despair, hinting at the unspeakable terrors they had witnessed in times past. The weight of their memories hung heavy in the air, and it was all Joel could do to endure the oppressive tension in the tent. He longed for a reprieve, a moment of solace to ease the pain of the present. With a heavy heart, he trudged out of the tent, searching for a sympathetic ear and a bottle to share.

The days that followed were a bleak repetition of agony and interrogation. Joel endured the ritual of having his wounds tended by the doctors and then being subjected to the same old questions posed by a trio of officers. Their inquiries pierced his soul, tearing at the fabric of his being. Memories of his captivity and the atrocities he had witnessed flooded his mind, and he struggled to maintain composure under their relentless scrutiny.

As he answered their questions, he realized one of the officers was a psychiatrist, Dr. Blackman. The man probed deeply, asking the most bizarre and inquisitive queries Joel had ever heard. He recounted the horrors of the prison camp, the escape, the brave Polish freedom fighters, the liberation of the POWs, and the death of the German prisoners. His heart weighed heavy with the knowledge that these memories would haunt him for a lifetime.

May 23, 1945, marked the momentous occasion of the Medal ceremony, a grand event that had been meticulously planned to honor the brave soldiers of the 3rd Army. The preparations were nothing short of magnificent; bleachers were erected, metal chairs were trucked in for VIPs and special honorees, and thousands of soldiers were transported to the venue. As far as the eye could see, tall poles stood erect, holding up speakers that would broadcast the ceremony's proceedings. MPs patrolled the area, ensuring that order was maintained amidst the bustling throngs of people.

Joel despised the grandiosity of such events, but he dutifully donned his new Class A uniform and rode with the other ex-Pows to the event field. Upon arrival, they were seated in chairs close to the grand stage, where thirty chairs had been set up on the floor. A colossal tent had been erected behind the stage, adding to the grandeur of the occasion. Joel's stomach churned with nerves; he had no idea why he was there, and the uncertainty of it all only added to his anxiety.

As the officers ascended the stairs to the stage, Joel's eyes widened in amazement. He had never seen so many General officers in one place! When the ceremony commenced, one after the other, the Generals took to the microphone, each extolling the virtues of their respective units and expressing their pride in being part of the 3rd Army.

Then, a hulking Major General approached the mic and bellowed, "Attention!" The sound of hundreds of boot heels coming together was deafening, like the roar of a thunderstorm. And then, in a voice that carried the weight of history, he proclaimed, "Now I have the honor of introducing the greatest General in the history of the United States Army. The commanding General of our 3rd Army, Lt. General George S. Patton!"

The air was electric with excitement as the crowd erupted in applause, their admiration for Patton palpable. Joel watched as the legendary General took the stage, his imposing figure cutting a commanding presence. It was a moment that would forever be etched in his memory, a testament to the courage and sacrifices of the men who fought and died for their country.

Joel was convinced that the resounding ovation he bore witness to would be recorded in the annals of history as the most deafening and enduring of all time. It reverberated through the air for what felt like an eternity, the thunderous applause causing the earth to tremble beneath his feet. Not a soul dared to cease the cheering until the flamboyant General, with an air of authority and power, lifted his riding crop high above his head and let out a deafening bellow.

"By damn," he roared, "this is the greatest field army ever assembled! We have the best damn officers and the best and bravest enlisted men ever. You men are the fightingest son of a bitches I've ever commanded! Commanding this Army will always be my greatest honor! We have fought long and hard. We have inflicted more damage on the Third Reich than any other soldiers in the Allied Expeditionary Force! We crushed the second-best trained Army ever, and now we are ready to go home. But I believe it will be another six or eight months before we get on the big boats headed to the States. I believe we will be tasked with running the damn Communist Red army out of Germany and Poland, back across their border where they belong. I won't be happy until those barbaric bastards are back in Moscow. So, stay sharp, stay hard, because, by God, I'll be seeing you sons of bitches soon!"

Joel was left utterly dumbfounded by the larger-than-life figure of Patton; his presence seemed to fill the entire space. He knew he would never forget that moment, the sheer force of the General's personality leaving a deep impression on him. And yet, amidst all the excitement, the award ceremony was soon underway.

As the names of Major Wood and the ex-POWs were called out, Joel couldn't help but feel a sense of pride and admiration for the incredible tales of bravery that were being recounted. The commanding General of the 179th Infantry Division spoke of their harrowing capture, daring escape, and stunning return to liberate the prison camp. Joel listened intently, amazed by the General's words which painted them as true heroes - almost as if they were straight out of a John Wayne film. But in reality, they were just tired, hungry, and scared soldiers who were merely doing their job.

After the Major was awarded the Silver Star, it was Joel's turn to receive recognition for his service. He, along with Sgt. Sanchez and Pvt. Hedman were each awarded the Bronze Star, a testament to their bravery and dedication in the face of danger. In recognition of his exceptional service, Pvt. Hedman was promoted to the rank of Corporal, while Joel was promoted to Staff Sgt. To top it off, all the enlisted men in the group were given the Combat Infantry Badge, a symbol of their courage and sacrifice in the line of duty.

Joel thought that was the end of it, but to his surprise, he was also given a second Purple Heart, a recognition of his remarkable resilience and fortitude in the face of adversity. However, it was the Combat Infantry Badge that truly held a special place in his heart - a badge that he was truly proud to have earned.

As they were about to leave the stage, the General announced one final citation. It was for PFC Andrew Snow, who had heroically sacrificed his own life on the night of the escape to save his fellow soldiers from being recaptured or killed. The posthumous award of the Distinguished Service Medal was a solemn reminder of the ultimate sacrifice that some soldiers had made in the line of duty.

As they made their way off the stage, a Sgt. motioned for them to return to their seats. Sgt. Sanchez simply ignored the comment and started walking back toward their tent, and the other enlisted men followed suit. It was a small act of defiance, a testament to their unbreakable bond as brothers in arms.

As the sun began to set, Major Wood prepared to leave for Nuremberg. Joel watched as the Major stepped onto the plane, feeling a sense of admiration and respect for the man who had led them through so much. The next morning, Joel bid farewell to the enlisted men he had shared so much with over the past months. Though he had never been particularly close to any of them, he felt a sense of camaraderie with each and every one of them and knew that he would miss their company.

As the rest of the men boarded the plane to London, Joel was offered a flight to Paris by the travel officer. But Joel's distrust of flying made him decline the offer, "Sir, unless you give me a direct order, I'm not getting on a plane! I've seen too many of them fall out of the sky!" he said. The travel officer couldn't help but chuckle at Joel's reluctance but agreed to arrange for him to take a train the following day.

When Joel arrived in Paris, he was taken to see a surgeon. The doctor examined the wound on Joel's chin and recommended a skin graft, which he would perform the following day. Though Joel had never been fond of doctors, he reluctantly agreed to the procedure. The next morning, as the sun was just beginning to rise, Joel felt a surge of anxiety and fear as he prepared to undergo surgery. Despite his misgivings, he lay still as the doctor performed the procedure, removing a small piece of skin from Joel's buttocks and carefully stitching it over the wound on his chin.

Joel had spent a full eight days traversing the streets of Paris, although not always for leisurely purposes. When he wasn't conferring with the hospital staff or engaging in discourse with a mental health specialist, he was indulging himself in the nightlife of the City of Lights. It was there that he discovered the French prostitutes to be of a wilder and more carnal nature than anything he had ever encountered before. They would cast their modesty aside and reveal themselves in the most unambiguous of ways. With grins upon their faces, they would leap upon him and proceed to bounce around in a most delightful fashion.

But despite the distractions, he found himself unable to find solace in sleep. During the witching hours, the darkness would call out to him, and all the haunting memories of war would come flooding back. He would see, hear, and smell the unspeakable horrors of battle, leaving him more fatigued than when he had lain down.

The psychiatrist he was made to see probed him with a litany of questions, ranging from his earliest recollections to the present day. He informed Joel that he was suffering from a severe case of battle fatigue, which could only be remedied by sharing his battlefield experiences with another. This sparked a furious response from Joel. He rebuked the idea that he was afflicted and in need of assistance, "I didn't see or do anything every other soldier saw, and I'm not sick in the head. I don't need your damn help, so just leave me alone!" he said.

After being cleared for departure by the surgeon, Joel boarded an aging Navy Cruiser, elated to be departing the continent but equally apprehensive about his impending reunion with his mother and the rest of his family. He feared that he would no longer be able to comport himself in a way that they would find familiar, leaving him feeling stranded and alone in the world.

The ancient vessel that ferried Joel across the vast Atlantic was a lumbering, outdated behemoth that required seven full days to traverse the sea. Once they had arrived, the soldiers were informed that they were to be taken to Fort Hamilton, a military installation situated in the heart of Brooklyn. Here they would receive their orders for future deployments, as well as have their travel accommodations arranged.

On the day of their arrival, the uniform of the day was Class A, so Joel dressed accordingly and strode purposefully toward the main deck. It was then that his new, temporary Company Commander spotted him and beckoned him over. The Captain appeared stern and unyielding, his face twisted into an expression of anger and indignation.

"SSgt, where the hell are your medals?" barked the officer.

Joel, taken aback by the suddenness and ferocity of the Captain's words, hesitated before replying. "Sir, I hate wearing the damn things; I never did anything to deserve them."

This only served to further enrage the officer, who exploded into a fit of anger. "How dare you make light of those medals? There are thousands of men buried over there that would love to be walking off this boat. So, don't you dare belittle what we did? Do you know, SSgt., that out of the entire 3rd Army, only 127 men were captured by the Nazis? If you know it or not, you have become a member of an elite club. So, get the hell back in there and put those damn medals on; they're not just for you; they're for all of us!"

With his words still ringing in Joel's ears, he retreated back below deck to retrieve his medals. As he affixed them to his uniform, he couldn't help but feel a deep sense of shame and remorse for having slighted the honor of those who had fought and died alongside him. He resolved then and there to never again denigrate the valor of those who had made the ultimate sacrifice in service of their country.

As soon as Joel and his fellow seafarers disembarked from the vessel, he rushed over to the grizzled old Msgt. Riley, with whom he had forged a fast friendship during their oceanic voyage to the United States. "Master sergeant," Joel implored, "could I request a favor of you?" Riley, unperturbed, replied, "Of course, kid. What do you need?" Joel proceeded to inquire, "Would you kindly take charge of my duffel bag? I have the hankering to see what all the fuss is about in the Big Apple!" The wizened veteran chortled heartily before granting Joel's request, cautioning him, "Okay, son, but don't go getting yourself in a tight spot!"

Joel set off on foot, ambling for about half an hour before two salty sailors in an antiquated pickup truck offered him a lift. Inquisitive, one of them queried, "Where are you headed, son?" Joel responded, "I figured I'd take a gander at downtown New York City." Both seamen guffawed boisterously, with one of them quipping, "We're aiming to get as close as we can to downtown, but brace yourself; it's going to be a throng!" Puzzled, Joel inquired as to why the area would be so congested. The younger sailor elucidated, "This is purported to be the grandest coming home bash in the city's history. It'll be one hell of a party!"

Growing up, the Fourth of July had always been a modest affair for Joel, marked by fried chicken and a couple of watermelons enjoyed at a picnic. However, upon arriving as close to downtown as possible with his new companions, Joel was utterly stupefied. He had thought he had seen masses of soldiers before, but this was unlike anything he had ever witnessed. The sea of humanity before him seemed to stretch as far as the eye could see, surpassing his wildest imagination.

The three young men wasted no time in their search for a libation, and within moments, they had procured a bottle of Kentucky whiskey. With their newfound elixir in hand, they began weaving their way through the frenzied crowd. The sheer volume of handshakes and hugs they received was almost overwhelming, causing them to blush with embarrassment. However, the experience was not without its benefits, as a horde of women descended upon them, showering them with kisses on their lips until they were left feeling dizzy and disoriented. Joel had never before indulged in such revelry, losing himself in a whirlwind of dancing and making out with countless women.

When he finally stumbled upon Fort Hamilton and Msgt. Riley, Joel was in a sorry state. The older soldier took pity on him, guiding him to his bunk, where he slept like the dead for a full day and night. By the time he awoke, Joel was already a day late in the process of learning about his next assignment. Despite his trepidation about potentially being shipped off to California to fight the Japanese, Joel was no longer dreading it any more than the prospect of returning to

Texas to see his family.

Hundreds of soldiers milled about, all in the same boat as Joel, awaiting their next orders. Yet, despite the throngs of servicemen, Joel was granted priority treatment due to his status as an ex-POW and decorated veteran. This attention left him feeling deeply embarrassed, yet he could not deny the privileges it afforded him. Eventually, after waiting in numerous lines, Joel came face-to-face with the officer who would be issuing his duty orders. Without so much as a word, the officer checked his ID before presenting him with a small envelope containing his orders, as well as a large blue envelope that had been securely sealed with tape bearing the warning "do not open." Joel was instructed to present it to his new company commander as soon as he arrived at his new fort, and with that, he set off into the unknown.

Joel stepped out of the small office, orders in his hand. The crumpled paper had seen better days, much like Joel himself. He was relieved to see that he would be returning to Fort Polk, a place he knew and had enjoyed. The thought of going back to a familiar place, where he had made some good memories, brought a small sense of comfort to him.

However, the relief was short-lived as he thought about Perdue and Phinn. He didn't know where Perdue was or if he was even alive. Joel's heart sank at the thought of his comrade being lost or worse. Then he thought about Phinn, the life of the party who loved to brag. Joel still couldn't believe that Phinn was gone. It was hard for him to accept the reality of his death, even after all he had seen during the war.

Joel's thoughts turned to guilt as he pondered why he had survived when so many better soldiers than he had perished. He couldn't shake off the feeling of responsibility and shame that he felt for being alive. The weight of loss and tragedy was too much for him to accept.

When Joel arrived at Fort Polk, he expected to feel happy and relieved to be back at a familiar place. But instead, he felt even sadder. The memories of the past came back to him, and he couldn't help but feel that he had lost a part of himself during the war. He wondered what would come next for him; with only five months left on his enlistment, he knew that the Army would have to extend it before shipping him off to fight the Japanese. He didn't want to go, but he wasn't afraid to either. The thought of going back into battle didn't scare him as much as the idea of not having a purpose beyond the war.

Part Two

Fort Polk bustled with activity as new draftees were trained and returning veterans from Europe were processed. Joel found himself assigned to a barracks in close proximity to the main gate and instructed to report to Major Branscum, the retention officer, on Tuesday at 8 in the morning. With three days to spare, he hitched a ride to town, hoping to revisit the nightclub he and his buddies used to frequent. But as he looked around the familiar surroundings, his thoughts turned to Phinn, and he felt a surge of anger at himself for even considering drinking there, knowing full well that Phinn had lost his life in France. So, he quickly caught a ride back to the base and stayed put until the day of his appointment with Major Branscum.

As he made his way to headquarters on that fateful Tuesday, Joel couldn't help but ponder the various outcomes that might arise from this meeting. Three possibilities came to mind: first, he might be forced to extend his enlistment for the duration of the war. Second, he might be offered the opportunity to reenlist, an option he had been considering. Or third, he might be assigned to a new unit, with his military future to be discussed at a later time. These possibilities weighed heavily on Joel's mind as he prepared to face whatever lay ahead.

As Joel waited for his meeting with the retention officer, he was approached by a Pfc. who he had served with briefly in Germany. They exchanged a few words and as the Pfc. noticed the blue envelope in Joel's hand, he exclaimed, "A blue one, SSgt. you're one lucky son of a bitch." Before Joel could respond, he heard his name being called from inside the office. He promptly marched to the desk, saluted, and gave his name and serial number. Major Branscum barely returned the salute but located Joel's file and informed him that there were a few documents to sign in the outer office before leaving.

After signing the necessary paperwork, Major Branscum laid out Joel's next few days of out-processing: a hospital exam the next morning, followed by paperwork at headquarters building 3, and discharge on Friday. Joel was in shock and asked why he was being sent home early when he still had nearly five months left on his enlistment. The Major's response left him reeling: "Why of course, it's because of your 100 percent disabled status. You did know about your rating, didn't you SSgt.?"

Joel couldn't believe what he was hearing. He had been completely unaware of any disability rating, and the news hit him like a ton of bricks. The Major's words swirled around in his mind as he tried to make sense of it all. How could he be disabled? He had been in the best shape of his life when he left for the war. As Joel stood in front of the officer's cluttered desk, he felt absolutely dumbfounded.

His face turned as white as a ghost, drained of all color and life after hearing the Major's words. "Sir, I don't believe either of my injuries warrant a disability rating," he said, almost pleadingly. The Major swiftly glanced over Joel's file and responded, "You're right about that, soldier. Your discharge will be based on mental health concerns. Don't forget to sign those forms on your way out." The weight of these words crushed Joel completely, leaving him feeling lost and alone.

After leaving the hospital, he made his way to the parade ground, where he slumped down and stayed for hours on end until the sun set and the stars came out. For the rest of the week, there was no grand send-off for the departing soldiers; they simply lined up and received their DD214 and separation pay before being sent on their way. Once again, Joel found himself a civilian, but he didn't know where to go or what to do. He knew he didn't want to return home just yet.

Joel remained in Monroe, Louisiana, for the next eleven days, indulging in a steady diet of hamburgers and milkshakes and catching up on the new movies. But each night, he drowned his sorrows with alcohol and chased after women. Despite having planned to stay for a month, he became increasingly restless and longed to see his family. He decided to lie and tell them that the Army had more than enough soldiers and was sending veterans from Europe home early. It was a flimsy excuse, but it would have to do.

Joel loaded up his duffle bag with all his belongings and donned his new civilian clothes before making his way to the train station. However, he was told that there was nothing available for the next three days going to Texas, which was where he wanted to go. His impatience grew as he had already made up his mind to go home. He decided to hitch a ride instead and made his way to the restroom to put on his Class B uniform. Joel had never before used his uniform to get a favor, but he figured it might help him get a ride quicker.

As he walked along the highway, it didn't take long for an old red semi-truck pulling a stock trailer to stop in front of him. The driver was an old Indian man with a wide smile on his face. Grateful for the ride, Joel hopped into the cab and thanked the driver. The old man asked him where he was headed, to which Joel replied, "I'm on my way home to Lorenzo, Texas, sir."

The driver, whose name was George Washington Halfcrow, admitted that he had never heard of Lorenzo before. However, he was transporting some racehorses to New Mexico and reckoned he could find his way to Joel's hometown. Joel tried to decline the offer, insisting that he didn't want to inconvenience the man. But George just laughed and replied, "Don't you worry about a thing, young man. I'll get you home safe and sound." And with that, the old truck rumbled back onto the highway.

Joel sat by the window of the old truck, gazing out at the passing scenery and pondering what awaited him at home. It was then that Halfcrow broke the silence. "Son, I saw your Combat infantry badge. Europe or the Pacific?" he asked. Joel replied, "Europe." Halfcrow nodded and said, "Me too. I was a code talker in the Great War in France, you know."

Joel was surprised by this revelation and nodded respectfully. But then they both fell into a comfortable silence; each lost in their own thoughts as the truck rumbled along the highway. Joel was so deep in thought that he eventually dozed off.

When he woke up, he noticed that the truck had slowed down and turned off the highway. He rubbed his eyes and peered outside to see that they had stopped at a large truck stop. Joel turned to Halfcrow and asked, "Where are we?"

Halfcrow grinned and replied, "Fort Worth, Texas. I need to take a leak and maybe dump a gallon of coffee while you fill 'er up. After that, we'll grab some grub and hit the road again."

Joel nodded and set to work, filling up the truck with gas. He checked the oil and air pressure in the tires, making sure everything was shipshape. Once he finished, he headed to the truck stop to grab some snacks and drinks. He asked Halfcrow if he wanted anything, and the old man replied, "Nah, I already got us some food. You go ahead and get yourself a drink. I'll take care of the horses, and then we'll chow down together."

Joel smiled gratefully and went inside to grab a Coke. As he stood in line, he couldn't help but feel a sense of camaraderie with Halfcrow. Despite the age gap and differences in their experiences, they were both veterans who had seen their fair share of war. And now, they were on a journey together, headed towards Joel's home.

Joel sat in the truck, munching on the delicious BBQ sandwiches Halfcrow had given him. As he savored the taste, he offered the old man a Dr. Pepper, but he declined, opting for his coffee instead. After they finished eating, Joel cracked open a Blue-Ribbon beer and offered one to Halfcrow. The old man hesitated for a moment before accepting, explaining that he hadn't had a beer in years.

As they drank, Halfcrow began to open up to Joel, revealing the deep scars left by his time as a code talker in the Great War. "Boy, I told you I was a code talker in the First War. I saw and did things no man should do. When I came home, my mind was so twisted I had lost my vision. I couldn't see a future because my thoughts were stuck in the past. For three years, I rambled and roamed, I'm sure I would be long dead, but I met a wise man. He saw my troubles and that my spirit was tied in knots. He told me the only way to free my mind was to tell someone what I had seen and done; to talk about it was the only way to be free of it. I learned how to talk, and it saved my life. You, Son, are a prisoner of your own war; if you speak, I will hear your words. We will probably never see each other again, so your story will go with me and not haunt you anymore for a while. But you will have to find someone to listen when it returns."

When Joel finished his story, Halfcrow nodded solemnly and placed a hand on his shoulder. "You're not alone, Son," he said. "Talking about it is the first step to healing. It won't be easy, but you'll find a way through. And when you do, you'll be stronger for it."

Joel thanked the old man for his wisdom and kindness, knowing that he would never forget this chance encounter on the road. As they drove off into the night, he felt a sense of peace settling over him, knowing that he had taken the first step on the long road to healing.

The old man said nothing more and climbed into his truck, and Joel, sensing the old man's silent command, followed him. They drove in companionable silence all the way to Lorenzo, with the wind whipping around them and the sun beating down on the dusty road. When they finally reached the intersection of the highway and the small dirt road that led to Joel's parents' home, George Washington Halfcrow pulled his truck over. Joel shook the old man's hand, expressing his gratitude and saying a heartfelt goodbye.

As Joel clambered out of the cramped truck cab, Halfcrow turned to him and imparted some words of wisdom, "Remember, son, you have to talk to live; you don't want the storm to follow you forever." The young man was struck by the old man's sage advice and felt as though he had just shared a ride with a truly Wise Man.

Joel's ancestry was a mixture of Cherokee and Irish, with his mother being a quarter Cherokee and his great grandparents both being full-blood Cherokee who had been born and raised on a reservation in Missouri. Despite their strong Christian beliefs, he always sensed that his grandparents held onto some of the old ways and beliefs that were part of their heritage.

As he shouldered his duffle bag and prepared to make the seven-mile trek home, Joel was suddenly struck with a deep longing for his grandparents and their Cherokee traditions. He briefly considered turning around and hitching a ride to Coal County, Oklahoma, to visit them, but he knew that his family was eagerly awaiting his arrival. With a heavy heart, he set off on foot, determined to reconnect with his roots and hold onto the wisdom that the old man had shared with him during their journey.

Joel trudged closer to home yet inexplicably felt his heart grow heavier with each passing step. The closer he got, the more he felt the crushing weight of sadness and loneliness bearing down on him. But just when he was less than a mile away from his destination, he was startled by the sound of hooves approaching. It was Clem Thomas, perched atop a majestic black mare that towered over Joel; it stood at least seventeen hands. He knew Clem well; the man always rode the finest horses, and Joel had groomed and cared for many of them in his time.

Clem greeted Joel warmly, taking his hand in a firm grasp and expressing his relief that he had finally made it home. He spoke of how hard it had been for Joel's family, especially his mother, with him being away for so long. He also mentioned how much he had missed Joel's fine work on his farm. But despite the kind words, Joel couldn't help but feel a deep-seated dislike for the man. He had seen Clem scream and curse at his father, Hubert Mills, and other workers too many times to count. Yet, despite his mistreatment, Hubert had always kept coming back to work for Clem because he paid them a quarter more per day than anyone else.

As Joel neared his family's front yard, he saw his older brother Josh staring in his direction. Josh started quickly toward the road but was stopped in his tracks by their father's voice and reluctantly stood and waited. Despite his inner turmoil, Joel couldn't help but feel a small sense of relief that he had finally made it home to his family. But as he drew closer, he knew that the challenges he faced would not be easily overcome, and he steeled himself for the trials that lay ahead.

When Joel arrived home, he saw that everything was still the same, just as he had expected. His father, Hubert, was a tough man who always insisted on having things his way, but Joel still respected and loved him deeply. He had heard his father say many times, "As long as you live under my roof, it's my way or the highway, so if you don't like it, hit the damn road." Joel knew that his father had a soft side, but he never dared to test it.

As Joel approached his family, he was warmly welcomed by his mother, Gladys, who held him tightly and cried tears of joy. His older brother, Josh, bombarded him with a barrage of questions, eager to hear about his experiences overseas. But it was his father, standing a few steps away, who caught Joel's attention. As they looked at each other, Joel felt like his father was reading his mind, seeing all the things he had gone through and the horrors he had witnessed. It made him uneasy, so he broke away from his mother's embrace and gave Josh a firm handshake before approaching his father.

For a moment, they stood there in silence until Joel reached out his hand to his father. Hubert grabbed his son's hand and pulled him close, enveloping him in a warm bear hug. Then he asked, "How have you been, son?" Joel felt a lump in his throat but managed to lie, "Just fine, dad, just fine." He knew that no one would ever understand the true extent of what he had experienced, and he didn't want to burden them with it anyway.

His father stood motionless for a beat before he uttered, "Josh, we best get back to work." The words hit Josh like a punch, "My gosh, Dad, Joel just got home!" he protested. But Hubert was unyielding. "I know he did, son," he said. "But them mules ain't gonna plow by themselves. Besides, your brother's probably starving." And just like that, the two men pivoted and vanished into the field.

Joel's mother took his hand and led him into their home. She retrieved a plate from the table and served him some cold fried chicken, cornbread, and a jar of buttermilk. Joel ate his meal in silence, lost in thought. When he finished, Gladys offered him a glass of sweet milk and a bowl of her famous vinegar cobbler. Overcome with gratitude, Joel kissed her hand and murmured, "Looks like I made it home after all."

As Joel savored his dessert, Gladys examined his hands and face. Her gaze fell on the numerous scars dotting his skin before she touched the prominent pale scar on his chin. "How bad were you hurt?" she inquired softly. Joel, reluctant to share the gory details of his ordeal, replied curtly, "Just a scratch." Gladys shook her head in disbelief. "Joel, you have a Purple Heart with an oak cluster," she reminded him. "They don't hand those out for scratches." Joel's tone grew defensive as he retorted, "I guess they did when it came to me!"

When Joel finished eating, he reached for a cigarette and found that he was out. He walked to his old bedroom and changed clothes. When he returned to the living room, he reached to the mantelpiece and took his dad's Prince Albert tobacco and papers and rolled several cigarettes. He kissed Gladys and said he needed to go help with the hoping. Gladys watched out the window as he headed to the field. Her earlier happiness was now shadowed with worry.

When Hubert and Josh returned, Gladys asked, "Where is Joel? He went to the field shortly after you. "Josh replied, "We haven't seen hide nor hair of him; I best go find him." Before Josh made it to the screen door, Hubert said, "He knows where the house is. Let's eat; we have work tomorrow." Josh was just finishing washing dishes when Joel arrived. He was filthy and soaked with sweat. He lay three cartons of Camels on the table and said, "I got each of you a carton." Josh and Hubert both thanked him as they made their way to the porch.

Joel ate a large meal of squirrels and dumplings, then washed his plate and joined his family outside. As soon as he sat down on the steps, Josh found he could not hold his questions in any longer. As he started toward Joel, Hubert let out a load huff. Josh ignored him and sat beside his younger brother, and questions spewed from his mouth. Hubert saw the pain in Joel's eyes. He looked at Gladys and said, "Are you ready for bed? I'm worn out." Gladys wanted nothing more than to sit with Joel, but she understood what her husband had meant, so she said good night and walked into the house. As soon as the lantern went out, Joel stood and walked toward the road in front of the house. Josh quickly followed.

As they made their way through the darkness, Joel asked, "Don't you happen to know where we can find a bottle?" Josh replied, "Sure, we can find something to drink over at Deerfield. Joel laughed and said, "How the hell would you know what's in Deerfield?" Josh just laughed and motioned for Joel to follow. Josh was full of questions about the war, how many Nazi bastards did you kill, what were the women like, did you get a lot of pussy over there? Joel turned to his favorite brother and said, "I'll answer all your questions later, but you tell me about Deerfield."

Josh was irritated by Joel's lack of answers, but he told Joel the story. "Joel, right after Mark joined the army, Dad started sending me over there to fetch him a bottle pretty often, I asked if you could go, but he didn't know you or mom to know for some reason. I've made friends with almost everyone over there." What made all this seem strange to Joel was that Deerfield was a small black community in the middle of nowhere; the Mills had worked side by side with most of the inhabitants, but usually black stayed with black, white with white. After walking several miles through plowed fields, they came to Deerfield. Josh didn't slow his pace but walked between the small houses like he lived there.

He walked up to the back door of one of the homes and knocked quietly. A young lady came to the door, and when she saw Josh, she said," Josh, you're too late, I'm out of liquor, and my boyfriend is in town, so you ain't getting nothing else either. "With that, she laughed loudly and said, "Mister Tom has a new batch; go see him," Josh said thanks and headed to the front of the next house. On the front step sat a very old, very large black man as dark as night itself. When he saw Josh, he said, "Hey, mister Joshua was your daddy; I pert near never see him no more."

They exchanged pleasantries for a moment then Tom said," All I have is calk beer, but it is fine if I do say so myself. "They followed him to a cellar, and as he started down the steps, he asked how much they wanted. Josh started to say a couple, but Joel interrupted and asked, "How much do you have? "Old Tom answered, "Eight bottles. "Joel said, "We'll take them. "Josh whispered, "It's strictly cash money over here, and I ain't got but sixty cents. "Joel just waved his hand and helped Tom up the steps. Tom handed each brother four beers out of his huge hands and walked back to his chair. Joel asked, "How much do we owe you?" Tom said, "Twenty cents each that will be $1.40. Joel said, "You're cheating yourself."

Tom smiled and said, "No, we're not to share this one." He took a bottle from Josh and popped the cork; he took a swig and held it out. Joel took it and had his pull off the bottle, then handed it to Josh. Soon the bottle was empty, so Joel paid old Tom, said their goodbye, and headed home. As soon as they were out of earshot, Joel laughed and said, "Do you have any idea what Mom would have thought if she saw us drink after him?" They shared a good laugh, opened two more beers, and walked on through the darkness.

The days were cold now; the Mills men were busy chopping cotton. This was the time of year they usually headed home to Oklahoma. Joel was anxious to go, and he thought his old stomping grounds might help the constant nightmares he was suffering from. The next weekend Josh asked Joel to go to town with him to see a movie and visit his girlfriend, Milly Cross. Joel was glad to get away from his parents for a while, and as soon as they got to town, he found the first bar they came to. While Josh and Milly enjoyed the movie, Joel got completely tanked. Josh had to help him to the car. As they drove Milly home, Joel popped his head from the back seat and said, "When are you love birds getting married? I think y'all should get married!" After dropping Milly off and making it home, Josh started to the front door, then noticed Joel wasn't following. said, "Come on, old-timer." Joel whispered, "I'm going to the tack shed; I'm not sleeping in momma's house drunk!"

The next day while everyone was busy, Joel snuck a blanket and pillow out to the shed and made it his hideout from prying eyes. Weeks passed, but Hubert never mentioned Oklahoma; everyone wondered why except Joel. He was lost to lack of sleep, hard work, and overdrinking. Every weekend was the same; Josh and Milly were having a good time while Joel got shit-faced. One evening Joel asked Josh to walk with him for a while. Josh knew it was just an excuse for Joel to get his bottle from behind the fence post where he hid it, but he walked with him anyway. After a while, Joel noticed they were standing in front of Clara Nuttall's house.

Memories swarmed Joel as he stood in the cold night air. He hadn't paid any attention to her place since he had returned and now saw that it was in complete disrepair. He asked Josh what the deal was. Josh answered, "Oh, she drowned the spring after you left. The crazy thing was trying to save one of her damn goats. She always was off in the head." Joel stood in shock for some time before Josh, not knowing what was happening, grabbed his arm and said, "Shit, I'm freezing, let's go home. "

Chapter 9 - The Nut House

In the coming months, Joel's family was plunged into a living hell. His once-vibrant personality withered away with each passing day, and he became increasingly withdrawn and sullen. He hardly ever came home to eat anymore and stopped going to town with his brother, Josh. Even when he did show up, he was uncommunicative and aloof, going through the motions of life with a detached air.

Gladys, Joel's mother, watched her son's slow decline with mounting anguish, her own health deteriorating in step with his. Joel's growing absence from the family's daily routines only intensified the feeling of isolation that had taken hold of the household. And when he did return, it was with an aura of melancholy that was impossible to ignore. Drunk and unkempt, with clothes that had gone unwashed for days, Joel's presence was like a dark cloud that hung over the family, suffocating them all.

Hubert, Joel's father, could no longer bear to watch his wife and son suffer in silence. One Friday morning, he confronted Joel as he was walking toward town, his voice heavy with the weight of all the pent-up frustration and despair he had been feeling for months. "Son," he said, his words laced with a mixture of anger and desperation, "I thought I knew the demons that are plaguing you. I was sure you could work through them. But I can't stand by any longer and watch your mother suffer. You have to get your shit together! You are slowly killing yourself and her too. I don't know what you will have to do, but get on with it, do you understand?"

Tears welled up in Joel's eyes as he looked at his father's troubled face. For a moment, he was transported back to a time when he was a child, and his father's presence had been enough to chase away all the monsters that lurked in the dark corners of his mind. And so, he stepped forward and took Hubert in his arms, holding on like a lost child in need of comfort and guidance. "Dad," he whispered, his voice thick with emotion, "you won't recognize me by supper time!"

And he was right. That evening, Joel joined his family for supper, and his appearance transformed beyond recognition. He was clean-shaven and had washed his clothes, a huge smile lighting up his face. Gladys could hardly believe her eyes as she watched her son laugh and tell jokes, his infectious smile spreading joy throughout the room. And when they moved to the porch, he sat by his mother's side, holding her hand and talking to her like he used to when he was a boy.

For a few fleeting moments, it seemed as if the old Joel had returned, his presence banishing the darkness that had threatened to engulf the family for so long. But as the weekend wore on, Hubert couldn't help but wonder how long his son could keep up the charade. He could see the strain in Joel's eyes, the telltale signs of a battle that was far from over. Only time would tell if Joel was truly on the road to recovery or if his transformation was just another temporary reprieve in a long and painful journey.

Gladys awakened from a restless slumber drenched in sweat, her chest heaving with fear. She held back a scream, not wanting to disturb her sleeping husband, Hubert. The nightmare had been so vivid, so harrowing, that she needed to check on Joel just to be sure he was safe. Without bothering to dress, she rushed to Joel's shed and peered inside. He was fast asleep, the rhythmic rise and fall of his chest providing some measure of comfort.

Her heart pounding in her chest, Gladys knew she needed to act fast. She needed to protect her son, no matter the cost. That's when a plan came to her, sudden and urgent. She moved to the small window next to Josh's bed and tapped softly. His face appeared bleary with sleep. Gladys whispered, "Get dressed and come through the window. Quietly, now." Josh's confusion was evident. "Mom, what's going on?" He asked. "I'm going to save your brother, whether he likes it or not," Gladys replied firmly.

With a sense of urgency, Josh quickly dressed and slipped out the window, his mother's determination and focus driving him forward. Gladys gave him clear instructions, telling him to lock the shed door with a pole barn nail and drive to Thomas's house to call Sheriff Hatcher.

"Hurry, son!" she urged, her voice urgent and tense. Josh had never seen his mother like this, her face set in a determined expression that brooked no argument. He ran quickly around the house and found a pole barn nail and shoved it into the hasp on the shed door, and was soon driving away.

Hubert's eyes shot open at the sound of a car leaving the yard. He sat up in bed, rubbing the sleep from his eyes. Gladys had lit a lamp and was holding a 22 rifle in her hand. Hubert's heart skipped a beat as he asked her, "Who left?" Gladys turned towards him, her face set with determination, and replied, "I'm going to save Joel, with or without your help. He's locked in the shed, and Josh has gone to get the Sheriff. Joel needs help, Hubert. He's killing himself right in front of us, and I won't let him go down that road. So, are you with me or not?"

Hubert stood up, pulling on his overalls. He looked at Gladys, his eyes softening as he spoke, "Of course, I'm with you. I love our son too." Gladys let out a deep sigh of relief and reached out to hold Hubert's hand. They waited together in silence, their hearts pounding in their chests.

When the Sheriff and his deputy arrived, Gladys and Hubert met them at the porch. The Sheriff removed his hat and shook their hands. He said, "I understand how hard this must be. Let's see how this goes." Gladys and Hubert led the way to the shed where Joel was being kept.

Joel was surprised to see his parents and the Sheriff so early in the morning. He was sitting on his bed, smoking a cigarette and wearing only his long johns. Gladys and Hubert stepped forward, but Gladys pulled Hubert back and approached Joel alone, closing the door behind her. She took him by the hand and said, "Joel, have I ever asked you for anything?" He shook his head, confused. Gladys continued, her voice cracking with emotion, "I'm not going to let you leave. You need help, son, and we can't give it to you. We've got the Sheriff and a deputy here, and we're signing for them to take you to a veteran's hospital. It's for the best, Joel. Please don't make this harder than it has to be."

Tears streamed down both their faces as Joel held his mother tight for a moment. He pulled away and said, "You know I would never make you cry on purpose, Momma. I am still your boy. If you want me to try the head doctor, I will. I thought I could beat this on my own, but I can't. Are they ready for me?" Gladys nodded, her heart heavy with the weight of what they had just done.

Gladys was overwhelmed by her tears, unable to utter a word, but her nod communicated everything Joel needed to know. They walked out together, hand in hand, braving the turmoil of emotions in silence. Once outside, Joel looked at his father and brother, his heart aching with the fear of being rejected by his own flesh and blood. "You two aren't too ashamed of me, are you?" he asked, hoping for the best but bracing for the worst. His father and brother rushed to him, embracing him tightly, their love and support undeniable. Josh's voice quivered as he spoke, "You're my best friend, little brother. I could never be ashamed of you." Joel felt a glimmer of hope and gratitude, but it was short-lived. In the next breath, Josh turned to the Sheriff and asked if they could stop in town for cigarettes, a stark reminder of the callousness of the world around them.

Joel didn't dare look back as he sat in the Sheriff's car, his mind spiraling with self-doubt and regret. The prospect of being admitted to a Veterans hospital in El Paso was daunting, to say the least. The thought of admitting to his mental struggles in front of his parents was a heavy burden, one that threatened to crush his spirit. When they arrived, Joel wished he had turned back, but it was too late. The hospital loomed large, its sterile halls and rooms a stark reminder of where he had ended up.

Joel was ushered into a room with sixteen beds, a shared shower and restroom, and eight other men from room seventeen. He smelled the food, but his appetite was gone. All he could think of was a drink, something to numb the pain and silence the voices in his head. The next day was no better. Joel tossed and turned, unable to sleep, his body shaking from lack of alcohol and caffeine. He forced down some toast and coffee, feeling sick to his stomach.

Dr. Huston Clark was waiting for him, a kind-looking man who spoke in a gentle tone. "Joel, I've reviewed your files, and I understand what you've been through. War, wounds, and capture at such a young age would take a toll on anyone. You have nothing to be ashamed of," he said, his words a balm to Joel's wounded soul. Dr. Clark explained the treatment options, urging Joel to start group therapy sessions and prescribing medication for his sleep and anxiety issues. He made it clear that Joel would have to stay until he was deemed fit to leave, a prospect that made Joel's heart sink.

The orderly led Joel to a small room where he was asked to remove his clothes. A young intern came in, examining him and commenting on his weight loss. Joel had no idea how much weight he had lost, but the intern's words were a sobering reminder. The young man said, "Well, you weigh 138 pounds; you weighed one eighty-two at your induction physical and one forty-four after being a POW for a month. So, I would assume you haven't been taking care of yourself. I'm putting you on extra rations until you are up to one seventy. Okay, let's get you your morning injection." Joel started to resist until the intern said, "Let's not get the orderly involved; you will get your meds one way or another!". "He was put on extra rations and given an injection, the promise of a long road ahead looming large in his mind.

Joel's heart raced as he weighed his situation. He knew that these people held his fate in their hands, but he wasn't sure if they could truly help him. Nevertheless, he made up his mind quickly. If he couldn't tell whether they were helping him or not, he would damn sure act like they were.

In the first few days, the hospital was a whirlwind of activity, grouping together men into classes based on the severity of their problems and the date of their arrival. Joel found himself thrown into the mix, his medication helping him with his sleep but unable to completely numb the pain of alcohol withdrawal and the bends at night. The days dragged on painfully, but eventually, the need for liquor eased, and he began to enjoy, or at least tolerate, the group meetings.

It took three long weeks before Joel finally stood and spoke. His mind raced as he thought of his loved ones - Josh, his parents, and even his grandparents. He wondered how his oldest brother Mark was and where his baby brother Bert had ended up after he had left home. He remembered Halfcrow's words about having to talk to live, and it spurred him on. Gladys had written with the news that Mark had returned from Germany and was working with Bert. He also learned that Josh and Bert had both married their girlfriends, and Mark was already engaged to an old girlfriend from Oklahoma. She sent love from herself and Hubert and promised to visit as soon as it was allowed.

As Joel began to find his place in the hospital, he formed a close bond with a soldier from Illinois named Lonnie Brown. They spent their smoke breaks together and shared a wicked sense of humor. Lonnie had been burned badly on Guam and had been in hospitals for months, just like Joel. Together, they became known all over the hospital, their laughter ringing out like a beacon of hope amidst the darkness.

One Sunday morning, after much pestering from Lonnie, Joel found himself in church. He hadn't been inside a church since before boot camp and had sworn never to enter one again shortly after witnessing combat. His faith in a merciful God had been shattered by the horrors he had seen. He was startled to find that the service was a Holiness one, not Catholic, Jewish, or anything he had expected. Nevertheless, he found himself drawn in by the sermon. Feeling like he was a child again, sitting beside his mother at a camp meeting.

But it was the testimonies of his fellow veterans that truly touched his heart. As they spoke of being brought out of hopeless situations in battle or overcoming deathly wounds, Joel felt a sense of camaraderie and kinship that he had never experienced before. When Lonnie praised God Almighty for letting him return to his mother, Joel felt tears prick his eyes. He was truly moved.

However, when he looked up and saw the pastor coming towards him, Joel couldn't handle it. He slid out from between the pews and out the door, his heart heavy with conflicting emotions. He had found some measure of peace in the hospital, but he wasn't ready to face his demons just yet.

Joel had been at the hospital complex for weeks now, and it felt like he was back in the military. The regimented routine was eerily familiar, with set meal times, mandatory exercise, and strict rules for leaving the premises. The absence of women made it feel even more like a barracks. But despite the familiar surroundings, Joel was finally making progress. His medication had been adjusted several times, and he was slowly putting on weight and feeling more like himself again.

One thing that surprised Joel was his newfound interest in attending church. It had been years since he had set foot in a church, and he had sworn off religion after witnessing the horrors of combat. But something about the Holiness services at the hospital spoke to him, and he found solace in the messages of hope and redemption. He wondered if it was just filling a void while he was stuck away from home.

All of this progress made Joel eager to leave the hospital and return home. He was overjoyed when he learned that his parents would be visiting the following Thursday, and he hoped that he would finally be able to go home with them. When he asked Dr. Clark about it, however, the doctor was cautious.

"Joel, I'm proud of the progress you've made, but you've only been here for three and a half months.

Let's see how your visit with your parents goes before we make any decisions about your discharge."

Joel couldn't believe it. He felt like he had come so far, and he was frustrated by the doctor's cautious approach. But he knew that Dr. Clark had his best interests at heart, and he reluctantly agreed to wait and see how things went.

When Thursday finally arrived, Joel was a bundle of nerves. He worried about how his father would react to seeing him in his current state, and he was terrified that he would break down in front of them. But despite his fears, he was also filled with hope. He had worked hard to get to this point, and he hoped that his parents would be able to see how far he had come.

As the orderly informed Joel that his parents were waiting for him in the reception area, his gut twisted into knots. Memories of his return home from the war flooded his mind, and the anxiety and unease that had plagued him back then seemed to engulf him as he walked the corridor. When he approached his parents, his mother's face glowed with a deep, unmistakable love that he had seen so many times before.

After exchanging brief greetings, Joel's stomach growled with hunger, a real craving for a juicy hamburger and shake. His father's smile wavered slightly as he led them to a magnificent, brand-new Packard waiting outside. Joel couldn't help but feel confused and asked his father where he had come up with this stunning car.

His father's voice was laced with a hint of annoyance as he explained how his mother had insisted on riding down with Doctor King and his family, despite his objections. They had all come to see Joel, but his father had made it clear that he needed Joel's permission first. "Dad," he said, "I'll be happy to see them as soon as lunch is over." Joel's answer was a resounding yes, and everyone laughed as they climbed into the car and made their way to the diner.

As they walked towards the restaurant, Joel insisted on paying for the meal, as well as the fuel and motel room. His mother looked at him with a mix of pride and confusion, wondering how he could afford such things without a job. Joel blushed and explained that he had been made to fill out some forms for military disability, which had helped him cover the expenses.

Lunch was a joyous affair, filled with laughter and smiles that eased the tension that had been building up inside Joel for months. As they arrived at the motel where his parents and their friends were staying, Joel caught a glimpse of the most beautiful girl he had ever seen.

He longed to meet her and daydreamed about how it would be to hold her and feel her warmth. But he knew it was impossible while his parents were with him. Fate was not on his side, he thought bitterly. And then, as if on cue, Hubert appeared with the Kings in tow. The girl was walking next to Dr. And Mrs. King. Joel finally realized it was their daughter Susan. The last time he had seen her, she had looked like a child. What a difference a few years makes, he thought.

Susan asked, "Dad, can we go bowling tonight? I've always wanted to try it." Doctor King said, "Probably Susan, but you should find your manners and say hello to Joel. You two remember each other, don't you?" When their hands touched, Joel felt a jolt of electricity shoot up his arm. He knew then that he had found a reason to fight, to recover, and leave this wretched hospital for good.

As the visit passed by in a blur, Joel found himself drawn to Susan's beauty and playful charm. Her touch set his heart racing, and he made up his mind to make her his. And as they said their goodbyes, Susan promised to see him again; she pledged to have a hero of her own. Joel clung to that promise, hoping it would keep him going until he was free.

Gladys and Hubert stayed until the last minute of visiting hours before going back to the motel to prepare for the trip back to Oklahoma. They told him they would be back as soon as they could afford it. He hugged each of them and said, "Don't waste your money; I'll be home before you know it." As soon as morning came, he was going to be the star patient at the hospital and be on his way home within a month. But as the night wore on, Joel found himself plagued by nightmares, sweating, and on the brink of screaming. His mind raced, and he tried to make sense of the chaos within him. Had Doctor Clark been right to caution him about his parents' visit? Was he too weak to handle it? Joel cursed himself for his carelessness, for letting his guard down in front of these people who were supposed to help him.

Come morning, Joel resolved to be more vigilant, to guard himself against anything that might delay his release. He would be the star patient, the one who showed everyone that he was ready to face the world again. And as he had watched his parents leave, promising to return soon, Joel knew that he would do whatever it took to make his dream of being with Susan a reality.

When Joel met with Doctor Clark, he made a conscious effort to conceal both his elation and agitation. He didn't want to raise any suspicion. As the doctor inquired about his visit, Joel put on a facade of normalcy, as if nothing had occurred out of the ordinary. However, beneath the surface, Joel was grappling with a flood of emotions, his heart brimming with joy and hope. For too long he had subjected himself and his family to a never-ending cycle of agony since returning from the war. But this time, something was different.

As he spoke with Doctor Clark about his visit, Joel couldn't help but feel a sense of relief. It was as if, this time, he had found a cure for his debilitating nightmares and mental anguish. But as he left the doctor's office, Joel knew he had to maintain an act of normalcy. He couldn't afford to raise any alarms, especially with the administration keeping a close eye on him.

A week later, Joel was summoned to the administrative department, where he met two unfamiliar men who proceeded to interrogate him with dozens of questions. Joel had no idea what was happening, but he thought it couldn't be good. The men offered no explanation, leaving Joel in the dark.

A week after the mysterious interrogation, Doctor Clark called Joel in for a meeting. The doctor seemed conflicted as he relayed the news that his supervisors had instructed him to ask Joel if he felt ready to leave. Joel knew better than to let his guard down. He understood the game being played, and he played along. After considering his response, Joel replied that he could function on his own. But Doctor Clark wasn't convinced.

He knew that Joel was too smart for his own good and that he had outsmarted most of the staff. He said, "Joel, I really like you, and I know you have been through hell itself, but boy, you are too smart for your own good. I have been ordered to let you leave even though I know you have just charmed most of our staff. You will be allowed to go home the day after tomorrow, but at least I swayed the boss into letting me make it mandatory for you to receive group therapy and medication until I approve its termination. Good luck, Joel. I hope you find the happiness you deserve."

Despite his reservations, Doctor Clark was ordered to release Joel. Joel left the facility with mixed emotions, grateful for the help he had received but unsure of what the future held. As he walked out into the world, Joel knew that he was still in the throes of a battle, a battle for his own mind. He was determined to win it, to find the happiness he deserved.

As the Trailways bus wheeled to a stop at the Ada, Oklahoma terminal, Joel's heart thumped in his chest like the beat of an ominous drum. The war had taken its toll on him, and his nerves were frayed from constant danger and uncertainty. But he was back home, eager to see his grandparents and the familiar comfort of his old house. More than anything, though, he longed to see Susan, the girl who had captured his heart during his confinement at the hospital. She had become an obsession for him, a beacon of hope in the darkness of depression.

Joel knew he had to find her to see if she felt the same way he did. He ran to Doctor King's office, hoping against hope that she would be there. But the receptionist informed him that the doctor was in surgery for the next few hours and Susan was still at school. Joel's heart sank, but he refused to give up. He headed to the high school, hoping to catch Susan on her lunch break. He left his suitcase with the receptionist, not bothering to wait for her answer.

As he sprinted towards the new high-school parking lot, Joel's mind raced. Where would Susan be? Would she even want to see him? His doubts swirled like a deadly storm in his head. But then he heard her laugh, the sound that had brightened his mood during the sleepless nights at the hospital. He ran towards it, desperate to see her.

And there she was, standing with another girl and three high-school boys beside a brand-new Chevrolet Coup. Joel felt a pang of inferiority as he looked at the well-dressed group. They were clearly from wealthy families, and Joel knew he could never compete with their affluence. He turned to go, feeling ridiculous for thinking that Susan could ever be interested in him. Perhaps he had lost touch with reality.

But then one of the boys spoke up, and Joel froze. They had noticed him staring. He felt his face flush with embarrassment, ready to slink away. And then Susan's voice rang out, loud and clear. There's my hero!" she exclaimed. Joel's heart leaped, and he turned to see her running towards him. As she leaped into his arms and kissed him, Joel felt all the willpower drain from his body. He was defenseless against her will, and he knew that he would follow her anywhere, no matter where, no matter the cost!

Chapter - 10 Back in Oklahoma

As Joel parted ways with Susan on the school grounds, he set out on a journey towards Lula, Oklahoma, his childhood home. His mind was preoccupied with thoughts of his grandparents, whom he had missed dearly over the past four years. The road was long and arduous, and Joel trudged along for nearly eight miles before he finally managed to catch a ride with a local family headed back to Coal County.

The ride was cramped and chaotic, but Joel was grateful for the company nonetheless. As he expressed his gratitude to his fellow passengers, he heard a familiar sound that stirred a deep nostalgia within him. It was the distinctive bark of Cruncher, his grandfather's faithful hound. Without hesitation, Joel dashed towards the tidy yard that led to his grandparents' home.

As he sprinted up the driveway, he almost collided with Cruncher, who was caught off guard by Joel's sudden appearance. The hound was quick to recognize his old friend, however, and bounced around him with joyous abandon. Joel dropped to the ground and engaged in a playful wrestling match with his beloved companion, relishing in the simple pleasures of homecoming.

It wasn't long before Joel's grandmother emerged onto the porch, her hand shading her eyes from the blazing sun. She called out, unsure of who the visitor might be. Joel sprang to his feet and rushed to her side, enveloping her in a warm embrace. The familiar scent of her famous meatloaf escaped from the kitchen, and Joel felt a deep sense of contentment wash over him. He had finally returned home.

Over the next few days, Joel reveled in the simple pleasures of country life. He caught up on all that had transpired in his grandparents' lives over the past few years, regaling them with tales of his own adventures and his recent trip with George Washington Halfcrow. It was a time of reunion and renewal, a period of respite from the tumultuous world beyond. For Joel, it was nothing short of heaven on earth.

Joel was taken aback by the reluctance of his Cherokee relatives to speak of their ancient customs and beliefs. Nevertheless, those few days spent with them were some of the happiest moments he had experienced in years, and he was loath to bid them farewell. But his parents were eager to see him, and so he set off on the four-mile walk to their house, bidding his Cherokee kin heartfelt goodbyes.

The homecoming was a grand affair, with Joel's brothers Mark, Josh, and Bert, along with several neighbors, aunts, uncles, and cousins all coming to pay their respects. Mark, in particular, took Joel aside and expressed his pride in him, recounting his own experiences during the Battle of the Bulge and expressing his admiration for the bravery of Joel and his fellow soldiers.

Despite the pleading of his brothers to work with them in the oilfields, Joel had his sights set on something else - Susan. He quickly secured a job at the feed mill in Ada and rented a small house on Craddock Drive, all the while hoping to win the approval of Susan's father, Dr. King.

The road to winning over Dr. King was a long and arduous one, with Joel making a dozen attempts to gain permission to date, Susan. Finally, with Susan's graduation from high school only two weeks away and her eighteenth birthday three weeks hence, Joel found himself once again standing in the hallway outside Dr.

King's office, his nerves jangling with anticipation.

As Mrs. King slowly opened the door to her husband's office, Joel couldn't help but marvel at the grandeur of the room. Her husband was perched on a colossal armchair, facing the largest bookshelf Joel had ever laid eyes on in someone's private abode. Dr. King raised his head and met Joel's gaze with a stern expression etched across his face. "Please don't ask again, son," he spoke gravely. "The answer will still be no. If you persist in this pursuit, I will have no choice but to send Susan away to my mother's house in Ohio."

Joel's heart sank as he stood there, helpless and desperate. "Sir," he pleaded, "I care deeply for your daughter. I will work tirelessly to provide for her. Won't you ever believe me?" Dr. King let out a weary sigh and looked at Joel with a sad expression. "I believe every word you say," he replied. "You are a good, decent man. But boys like you should never go to war. You are a broken man, Joel, and you don't even realize it. Someone like Susan could destroy you without even realizing what she had done. You have seen things and experienced things that she could never fathom, and she, in turn, has lived a life that you may not want to comprehend. I have been friends with your family since before you were born, so please, don't make this any more difficult than it already is."

Joel left the King's house, feeling defeated and crestfallen. He knew that Susan was probably with her sister, laughing and playing without a care in the world. That was one of the many things he loved about her, her unbridled happiness. As he stumbled into the Broadway bar in Ada, he was lost in his thoughts, unaware of his surroundings. It had been months since he had touched liquor, but that first sip of beer tasted so good that it was soon followed by several more.

Around one in the morning, as Joel made his way towards the door, he was suddenly met by an old classmate, Marsha Burris. He hadn't seen her in years and wouldn't have recognized her if she hadn't spoken to him. They made their way back to a cozy booth and talked and drank until closing time. At that moment, Joel was glad for the company and the warmth of the alcohol. For just a little while, he could forget about his troubles and just be in the present moment with someone who knew him from a simpler time.

The following morning, Joel woke up to a throbbing headache, a reminder of the previous night's drinking binge. As he fumbled to silence his blaring alarm, he was startled to find Marsha lying next to him, her tousled hair framing her face. She let out a hearty chuckle as she noticed the expression on his face. "Boy, you look like you've seen a ghost," she teased. "That's not how a lady wants to wake up with her lover."

Joel knew he had to head to work, but he couldn't bring himself to leave without addressing the situation with Marsha. He took her hands in his own and spoke in a soft, apologetic tone. "Marsha," he began, "I've always liked you, and you're a beautiful girl, but my heart is set on someone else. I hope I haven't hurt your feelings." Marsha simply smiled at him and replied, "I understand, Mr. Mills. I'm a big girl, and who knows, maybe you'll change your mind. You know where my parents live. Bye, lover."

Joel made his way to the feed mill, his mind consumed with worry that somehow Susan or her parents would find out about his dalliance with Marsha. Over the next month, Joel only saw Susan twice, each time during his lunch break at the mill. She showered him with affection and promised that they would soon be together. But for Joel, the waiting was unbearable, and he found himself turning to smoking, drinking, and spending more time with Marsha.

Joel confided in Marsha about his plans to marry Susan, but she seemed content with the time they spent together. She was a delightful Choctaw woman, easy to talk to, and always up for a good time. However, deep down, Joel knew that he was using her, and he felt guilty for not being able to end their fling.

On a Friday evening, when the sun was gradually sinking into the horizon, Joel was ready to head home after a long day at work, eager to embrace the weekend with open arms. As he approached his boss's office to collect his pay, his heart thumped with apprehension when his boss summoned him, saying he had an urgent phone call waiting for him. Joel's mind raced as he speculated on the possible reasons for the call. He feared that perhaps one of his parents had fallen ill or that there was some other calamity that demanded his immediate attention.

But as soon as he heard Susan's melodious voice on the line, his anxiety evaporated like a dewdrop in the morning sun, replaced by a rush of exhilaration that coursed through his veins. "Sweetheart, my parents are out of town until Monday. Can you meet me in Shawnee tonight? I've had one of my friends drive me up here," she said in a soft, tender tone that made Joel's heart skip a beat.

Overwhelmed with excitement, Joel scribbled down the address she gave him, then bolted out of the office and headed home. He quickly shaved and showered, his mind awhirl with anticipation and nerves, and then rushed to his car, his fingers fumbling with the keys as he tried to start the engine.

When he arrived at the Neon Lounge nightclub, he was taken aback to discover that Susan had invited him to such a risqué establishment. Doubts and apprehensions gnawed at his mind, but as he sat in his car, double-checking the address she had given him, he saw her beautiful face smiling at him through the windshield, and all his doubts vanished in an instant.

He leaped from the car and enfolded her in his arms; their bodies pressed together in a passionate embrace. After what felt like an eternity, they reluctantly pulled away from each other, their hearts still racing with desire. But Joel knew that he couldn't let his passion cloud his judgment. Susan was only eighteen, and her father had strictly forbidden their relationship. As he stepped back, Susan pulled him closer and kissed him again and again, her lips soft and warm against his.

"Let's go in and dance awhile; I've never been in a club before," she said, her eyes sparkling with excitement. Joel hesitated, knowing that it was a risky move, but he couldn't bear to deny her anything. He took her hand, and they walked into the club, the dim lights and throbbing music enveloping them in a haze of sensuality and desire. As they danced, Joel knew that he was playing with fire, but he couldn't resist the temptation of being with Susan, even if it was only for a few hours.

Susan seemed to take it all in stride. She sauntered up to the bar and ordered a drink, then followed Joel onto the dance floor, moving with a fluid grace that made it seem like she had been there a thousand times before.

As the night wore on, they drank and danced and talked, lost in their own world of passion and desire. But as the evening began to wind down, Susan suggested they grab a hamburger at the bar, her eyes glinting mischievously as she revealed that she had plans for later.

Joel couldn't help but wonder what she had in mind as they ate their hamburgers in silence, the air thick with unspoken desire. He hoped she didn't want to meet up with her friends; he wanted her all to himself tonight.

Finally, they left the bar and made their way to Joel's car, but before he could ask any questions, Susan began giving him directions. They led straight to the Cinderella Hotel, the nicest place in Shawnee. Joel's heart thumped with a mixture of excitement and apprehension. "Are you sure you know what you're doing? You're only eighteen," he asked, trying to keep his voice steady.

But Susan just growled playfully at him and said, "If you think of me as a child, take me home; if not, then let's go inside." Joel knew there was no turning back now. He paid the exorbitant fee for the room, knowing that he would have paid much more if it meant being with Susan.

As they stepped off the elevator and entered the room, Joel was taken aback by the sheer opulence of it all. The plush carpets, the ornate furniture, the soft lighting that bathed everything in a warm, golden glow. He felt like he was in a dream, a place where anything was possible.

But Susan broke his thoughts when she said, "Sweetheart, why don't you shower first if that's alright with you." Joel nodded, grateful for the chance to clear his head and gather his thoughts. As he stepped into the shower, he couldn't help but wonder what the rest of the night held in store for them.

Joel found himself entering the restroom with a sense of urgency, like a young lad on a mission. As he emerged, he was met with Susan's silent presence, her fingertips grazing his naked chest, sending shivers down his spine. In her other hand, she held a small satchel that had escaped his attention before. After indulging in a quick smoke, he shed the towel from around his waist and slipped beneath the covers, extinguishing the bedside lamp. The ensuing minutes stretched on interminably as he pondered how much he would have to explain to Susan.

And then, like a vision, Susan glided into the room, leaving a trail of light in her wake. Adorned in an ivory-colored gown that hugged her every curve, she was a sight to behold. Joel had always known she was stunning, but he hadn't realized just how much of a woman she was until that moment. Her eyes were aglow, and her bosom was fuller and ampler than he had ever imagined. The hem of her gown was raised, revealing her long, toned legs, tanned to perfection. As she sauntered towards him, a coy smile graced her lips, and she flicked on the bedside lamp with a flick of her wrist.

Approaching his side of the bed, she leaned in and untied the straps of her dress, letting it fall away to reveal her breathtaking form. With a gentle tug, she pulled the silky fabric aside, and her supple bosom spilled out, the tan nipples hard and erect, matching the shade of her luscious locks. The dress continued to slide downwards, baring her entire being to Joel's gaze. With a graceful twirl, she stepped out of it, making a languid circle around the room, her hands running down the length of her body, tracing every inch of her curves. Joel was transfixed, unable to look away as she raised her arms overhead and explored herself with a delicate touch.

With delicate strokes, she traced small circles around her nipples, a sight that made Joel's blood boil with desire. As she approached the bed, he shifted over to make room for her, never before having witnessed such a woman in all her glory. She lay down on her side, tenderly caressing his face and kissing him softly, her fingers slowly wandering across his chest and stomach until she reached her destination. With an open hand, she teased and tantalized him until he could bear it no longer.

He moved to cover her with his leg, but she pushed him flat with a hand on his shoulder, then straddled him, keeping his hands firmly pinned beside his head. Their mouths met in a fierce embrace, and she rubbed her tanned breasts against his face until he found one, savoring the softness and the warmth. Finally, they came together as one, slowly and deliberately, their bodies moving in perfect synchronization. The primal sound that escaped her lips was both loving and medieval, a melody of passion that echoed throughout the room.

They moved in unison, like two people in a boat on rough waters, barely touching the surface of each wave. She took him all in, and their rhythm was flawless, a symphony of desire and pleasure that climaxed in a crescendo of ecstasy. As they lay there, entwined in each other's arms, she placed her head on his chest, still tenderly touching him with her hand. Then, with a hushed voice, she asked him a question that had been weighing on her mind for some time.

"Joel, do you remember a couple of months ago when you said I was too young for you?" she murmured. He responded softly, "Yes, I do, love."

Susan lifted herself onto an elbow, looking at him with intense eyes. "Do you remember I said that if you gave me a small chance, I would change your life forever?" Joel brushed a lock of hair away from her forehead, smiling as he replied, "I remember that, sweetheart. And you were absolutely right."

Time passed in a blur of happiness for Joel and Susan, who spent every moment together that they could find. However, their romance was not without its challenges. Susan's parents were not fond of their daughter's relationship with Joel, and Joel's own parents were equally unsupportive. Gladys and Hubert had made their disdain for Susan clear, claiming that the two were from different worlds and that Susan was too young and spoiled to make a suitable wife or mother. Joel did not take kindly to their opinions and made it clear that he did not wish to hear any more of their criticisms.

One Sunday, Susan sent a message to Joel, urging him to come to her house after church. She promised him wonderful news, but Joel was hesitant to visit Dr. and Mrs. King's home. As he walked up the path to the front door, Susan suddenly appeared, throwing herself into his arms and showering him with kisses. This was the first time she had acted so openly and affectionately towards him in broad daylight at her parents' home.

Joel held her at arm's length, asking hesitantly, "Have your parents finally come to terms with our relationship?"

Susan shook her head, grinning from ear to ear. "No, they haven't," she said. "But I made it clear to them that I'm over 18, and there's nothing they can do to control me. I told them I'm not going to Kentucky University as they did; I'm staying here and going to East Central College. We can see each other whenever we want, and they can't stop us."

Despite the obstacles they faced, Joel and Susan remained determined to be together. They knew that their love was worth fighting for, and they refused to let anyone stand in their way.

Joel concealed his disappointment behind a mask of enthusiasm, but deep down, he was devastated by the turn of events. This was not the plan he had meticulously laid out. He understood all too well that Susan's parents would now forever hold him in contempt, and he couldn't fault them for it. For the first time, he wondered if perhaps Susan was as immature as others had claimed.

But then, something shifted within him, and a wave of unfamiliar pleasure coursed through his body. He and Susan were inseparable, drawn to each other like magnets. It felt like a match made in heaven, and they couldn't get enough of each other. So when Susan confided that her parents would be out of town for the weekend, Joel was overjoyed. He arranged to leave work early at 4 pm, eager to make the most of their time together.

But fate had other plans. On Friday, as Joel drove toward Susan's house, he reflected on how his life had taken a turn since his days at the VA hospital. Despite the lingering nightmares and the guilt of surviving while others perished, he felt a newfound sense of happiness that he believed he didn't deserve.

As he approached the King's house, he noticed a brand-new blue Packard parked in the driveway. His curiosity was piqued; he couldn't imagine why it was there. But when he drew closer, the sight that greeted him was one he could never forget. There was Susan, unmistakable even from the back of her head, entwined in a passionate embrace with a boy he didn't recognize, right in the front passenger seat of the car.

The air seemed to freeze around him, and his heart sank like a stone in his chest. He couldn't comprehend what he was seeing. The joy he had felt moments before dissipated into thin air, leaving only a sense of betrayal and hurt in its wake.

He slammed his car into park and bolted towards the blue Packard with a feverish determination. His heart was pounding in his chest, and his hands trembled with a potent mixture of rage and anguish. He flung open the door, expecting Susan to scream and plead with him, but instead, she greeted him with an amiable smile that made his blood boil.

Without hesitation, he hauled her out of the car and shook her, his fury bubbling over like an overflowing cauldron. Susan took a step back and hastily began buttoning her blouse, a feeble attempt to cover up the evidence of her infidelity. He lunged into the car and dragged out the whimpering fool she had been with, his mind reeling with a torrent of violent impulses.

But before he could unleash his wrath upon the hapless boy, Susan grabbed his arm and implored him to stop. "There's no need to hurt him," she said softly. "We were just fooling around a little. He came to see my sister, and we ended up here after drinking some wine. You can't stay mad at me, Joel. Don't forget that you're a hero."

Joel didn't say a word as he stormed away, his emotions in turmoil. When he finally arrived back in Ada, he made a beeline for the Broadway bar and remained there until closing time, nursing his wounds and drowning his sorrows in an endless stream of alcohol.

Chapter 11 - Out Living His Smile

In the dim and weary hours of the night, he would find himself on this path more often than not, a ritual of sorts for the sixty days that followed. The haze of those nights would blur together in his memory, and there were moments when he'd awaken, uncertain of how he'd found his way home. And there, each time, Marsha would be - a presence as constant and haunting as the passing hours themselves. He had never extended an invitation, yet she remained, and he could not gather the courage to ask her to go.

He could see the longing in her eyes, a yearning for something he could not provide, something that was more than he could bear to give. He knew deep within that she deserved love far richer and more profound than anything he had to offer. And as the days went by, her belly began to grow - a silent testament to a truth he could not bear to confront. The question lingered, unspoken, in the space between them, a weight that he could not lift.

Then, on an unremarkable evening, Hubert was there, standing sentinel in the parking lot as Joel's shift came to its end. Joel was a shadow of himself, his skin pale and taut against his thin frame, a sight that brought shame to his heart as his father's gaze met his own. They shook hands, and at that moment, Hubert's eyes betrayed the worry he attempted to mask. With a strained voice, he told his son that Gladys had invited Joel to share a meal with them come the weekend. Yet, in the same breath, he promised to relay the message that Joel would be unable to attend until the following weekend.

As Hubert turned to leave, he paused, and with a weariness that seemed to speak for both of them, he implored, "Son, please find a way to mend yourself before then." And with those words hanging in the air, he disappeared into the night, leaving Joel to reckon with the echoes of his own existence.

Over the course of the following week, Joel made a conscious effort to resist the numbing allure of the bottle, to nourish his body with wholesome food, and to rise above the darkness that had been consuming him. Marsha, ever watchful, noticed a subtle shift in him, a glimmer of hope that the clouds were beginning to part. When Saturday arrived once more, Joel took care to bathe and shave, presenting himself to the world anew as he set off for Lula, where his parents and grandparents awaited him.

Gladys had prepared a veritable feast, the table laden with dishes that enticed the senses. And yet, as Joel began to partake in the meal, he became acutely aware of the gazes fixated upon him. He looked down and, for the first time, truly saw the tremors that ravaged his hands. Despite the tantalizing aroma of the food, his appetite abandoned him. Gladys, her heart heavy with concern, could not help but be overwhelmed by the sight of her once vibrant son, now a shadow of himself – his body gaunt, his eyes hollow, his skin taking on a sickly, waxen pallor.

The visit was fraught with tension, and as it drew to a close, Joel exchanged handshakes and embraced his mother and grandmother. Stepping into the front yard, he paused to light a cigarette, the smoke curling around him like a shroud. When he saw Gladys emerging from the back door, he wished he had gone straight to his car. She approached, her eyes searching his face, and said, "Joel, you look terrible, son. Are you taking care of yourself? I'm not going to have to send you back to the hospital, am I?"

Joel shook his head slowly, the words forming carefully in his throat. "Mom, this thing with Susan... it's taken a greater toll on me than I ever could have imagined. But it's in the past now; everything will be alright. I should have heeded your and Dad's advice from the start. I love you; I'll see you soon." And with that, he turned away, carrying the weight of his mother's worry alongside his own burdens, as he stepped back into the world that awaited him.

On the winding road home, beneath the watchful gaze of a setting sun, Joel's mind raced and finally settled on a course of action. The decision brought him a sense of relief and purpose he had not felt in a long while. He whispered to himself that it was time to act, to set his plan in motion without delay. For the ensuing days, he immersed himself in labor, volunteering to work double shifts at the feed mill. He avoided the dimly lit bars that once lured him in and devoted his attention to the delicate Marsha.

But when darkness fell, and sleep beckoned, the nightmares returned with a ferocity that shook him to his core. He could hear the harrowing screams and smell the acrid stench of burning flesh. The lifeless bodies of French children haunted his memory, a grim reminder of the lives he had taken in his first hour of combat. He couldn't help but question how many other innocent souls he had dowsed. The number weighed heavily on his conscience. With the rain of mortars that he had sent into the heart of French and German towns, he had witnessed firsthand the grim aftermath. Now, in the stillness of the night, the faces of the dead and dying were etched into his mind, refusing to fade away.

Two weeks into his newfound dedication, Joel informed his foreman that the coming Wednesday would be his last day at the mill. His departure was met with pleading, and the tempting offer of a pay raise, but Joel's resolve stood firm. His plans, he told his boss, were unalterable. And so, on that final Wednesday, after bidding farewell to his workplace, Joel made an unannounced visit to his grandparents and then his parents. He broke bread with Gladys and Hubert, and as the evening shadows grew long, they sat together on the front porch, trading stories and laughter over a shared pack of cigarettes, until the chill of the night air forced them inside.

With a tender kiss, Joel bid Gladys goodnight and retreated to the familiar streets of his town. Gladys retired to her bed, her heart warmed by the marked improvement she had witnessed in Joel's demeanor.

Hubert, however, remained awake, consumed by a worry that gnawed at him more than ever before.

As the first light of morning broke over the horizon, Joel awoke with a sense of purpose; there was much to be done in the ensuing forty-eight hours. He traversed the town with determination, selling his prized Plymouth, shotgun, and rifle. His next stop was the bank, where he withdrew the modest sum that constituted his entire savings. A friend working at the Ford garage became the new owner of his tools. With his affairs in order, Joel treated himself to a hearty meal before making his way back home.

A block from his destination, Joel's attention was captured by a weathered Dodge pickup that had been a constant fixture in the neighborhood since he had first arrived in Ada. The widow who owned the truck recounted how her late husband had driven it until his final day. She was confident that with a little attention, the old Dodge would be reliable once more. Joel agreed, but upon realizing he no longer had his own tools, he found himself in need of assistance. The kindly woman was more than happy to lend him her late husband's tools.

In just a couple of hours the old Dodge hummed to life. Joel returned the borrowed tools to the shed, wished the lady well, and proceeded to his small house, where he found Marsha waiting. They enjoyed an early dinner together before Joel proposed a visit to the movies. Marsha agreed, but a hint of intuition told her something wasn't quite right.

After the movie, they retired to Joel's home and lay down to rest. He held Marsha in his arms, enveloping her in his embrace until she feigned sleep. He then rolled over, and both were left to wrestle with their thoughts. Sleep was elusive, but eventually, it claimed them both. The following morning, as Marsha prepared for work, she observed Joel's serene face, still lost in slumber. She couldn't shake the feeling, however, that beneath the surface, a storm raged within him, one that might never truly subside.

When the first light of day kissed the horizon, Joel stirred from his restless slumber. With an unsettling sense of purpose, he climbed into his battered pickup and set out to find fuel for his journey. The pungent aroma of gasoline filled the air as the nozzle pumped the liquid lifeblood into the truck's tank.

Afterward, he sought refuge in the dimly lit confines of a pawn shop, its shelves cluttered with the remnants of other people's lives. There, he procured the most modest, inexpensive firearm he could find — a .22-caliber snub nose revolver. It may have been unassuming, but it would still do everything it was meant to do.

Returning to his home, a place that once held the warm embrace of love and laughter, Joel solemnly gathered the sum of his monetary worth. With his account drained and possessions sold, he counted out $727.00. It was a respectable sum, but he couldn't help but wish for more. He found an envelope and, in his unsteady hand, wrote a message to Marsha: "Take care of yourself. You deserve to be happy." With a heavy heart, he placed $712.00 inside, leaving it to be discovered on the small, worn dinner table.

With the burden of his former life left behind, Joel drove westward for more than three hours as the skies grew dark and pregnant with rain. A relentless deluge soon enveloped his truck, shrouding the world in a veil of water and reducing visibility to a mere whisper. Yet, Joel was not in a hurry, nor did he have a specific destination in mind. He held a steadfast belief that he would find what he sought, wherever it might lie.

The rainfall persisted through the night, only relenting when the sun began its ascent into the heavens. As the world slowly revealed itself, a sign on the edge of the road caught Joel's weary eye. He slammed on the brakes, jolting the truck to a stop. Peering into the rear-view mirror, he backed up and steered onto a narrow gravel path.

The torrential rains had left the road slick and treacherous, a muddy morass that threatened to swallow all who dared tread upon it. Several miles down this forsaken path, Joel brought his truck to a halt before a weather-beaten sign. At that moment, the heavens opened once more, releasing a fury of rain unlike any he had endured throughout the night. Undeterred by nature's wrath, Joel stepped out of his truck and ventured forth, walking down the sodden road with determination etched upon his face.

As the sound of the river reached his ears, Joel drew closer to examine the relentless flow. Just as the sign had foretold, the bridge lay in ruin, a victim to nature's fury. He stood in awe of the river's speed and power, a testament to the unstoppable force of nature. With a heavy heart, he retraced his steps back to his truck.

Before reaching the old Dodge, he paused and heaved the sodden bridge-out-ahead sign from the road's edge. Once inside the vehicle, he started the engine, its familiar growl a reminder of countless past journeys it had taken its former owners. Gripping the small pistol, he set off, the gun making the task of shifting gears awkward but not impossible. The slippery road limited his speed, but he felt confident it would be enough.

And then, the moment arrived. As the pickup hurtled toward the watery abyss, the report of the pistol was swallowed by the roar of thunder and the river's relentless roar. The truck disappeared beneath the swirling waters, its secrets locked away from the world.

Over a year passed before the truck's battered remains were unearthed by three teenage brothers, their hands searching the murky depths for catfish. The Dodge had been ravaged by time and water, yet its secret remained intact. As Joel had never registered the vehicle in his name, tracing its origins took some time. When the news finally reached Gladys and Hubert, they were devastated, though Hubert could not say he was entirely surprised.

In the aftermath of the somber memorial service, a young Indian woman approached Joel's grieving parents. Introducing herself as Marsha Burris, she revealed that she and Joel had been close friends. While Gladys was unfamiliar with her, Hubert recognized the name from his desperate search for his son. As Marsha and Gladys spoke, Gladys was overcome with emotion, her tears flowing freely. "I can hardly remember his face," she sobbed. "Oh Lord, I can't even remember his smile."

As the somber dusk settled upon them, Marsha and Gladys reluctantly began to part ways. The fragility of the moment hung in the air as Marsha reached out with her hardened yet tender hand to lightly clasp Gladys's arm. In a voice barely audible, she asked, "Would you mind if I were to visit you in a couple of days? I have something in mind that could, perhaps, ease the heavy burden that has befallen your heart." Gladys, her eyes brimming with unshed tears, merely nodded in affirmation before making her way to the waiting automobile, her every step echoing the weight of her grief.

Two days later, as the sun reluctantly peeked through the melancholy clouds, Marsha, true to her word, found herself standing at the doorstep of the

Mills' residence. A hesitant knock came through the old wooden door. Hubert, his face lined with the sorrow of recent events, opened it to let her in. With a solemn nod, he stepped aside, allowing her to navigate the dimly lit hallway leading to the dining room.

There, at the head of the table, sat Gladys, her once vibrant eyes now hollow and distant. Since the funeral, she had scarcely moved from that very spot as though rooted in place by the gravity of her loss. Marsha approached her, and in a voice that carried both empathy and determination, she spoke, "Mrs. Mills, I'd like to introduce you to my son, Junior Burris."

Her words seemed to strike both Hubert and Gladys with a shared realization. In an instant, Hubert hurried around the table, his movements urgent and deliberate. Together, he and Gladys found themselves on their knees before the small boy who stood before them. He was a child of deep, dark complexion, his round face framed by hair and eyes as dark as the coal that lay beneath the earth. But as they spoke to him, something remarkable occurred.

A smile—so bright, so unexpected—spread across the boy's face, and it seemed as if, for the first time in days, the shadows that had claimed the Mill's home began to recede. It was a smile they had thought they would never see again, a smile that whispered of hope amidst the darkest of times. And in that single, fleeting moment, hope was rekindled within the hearts of Hubert and Gladys Mills.

Made in the USA
Middletown, DE
09 June 2023

31998125R00106